PRODUCING PROSPERITY

PRODUCING PROSPERITY

WHY AMERICA NEEDS
A MANUFACTURING RENAISSANCE

Gary P. Pisano
Willy C. Shih

HARVARD BUSINESS REVIEW PRESS

BOSTON, MASSACHUSETTS

No part of this publication may be reproduced, stored in or introduced into a
retrieval system, or transmitted, in any form, or by any means (electronic,
mechanical, photocopying, recording, or otherwise), without the prior
permission of the publisher. Requests for permission should be directed to
permissions@hbsp.harvard.edu, or mailed to Permissions, Harvard Business
School Publishing, 60 Harvard Way, Boston, Massachusetts 02163.

Library of Congress Cataloging-in-Publication Data

Pisano, Gary P.
    Producing prosperity : why America needs a manufacturing renaissance /
Gary P. Pisano and Willy C. Shih.
        p. cm.
    Includes bibliographical references.
    ISBN 978-1-4221-6268-2 (alk. paper)
    1. Manufacturing industries—United States—Management.   2. Industrial
management—United States.   I. Shih, Willy C. II. Title.
    HD9725.P57 2012
    338.0973—DC23

                                                                    2012015530

The paper used in this publication meets the requirements of the American
National Standard for Permanence of Paper for Publications and Documents
in Libraries and Archives z39.48-1992.

For Alice and Julie

Contents

Prologue: Does America Need Manufacturing?   ix

1. Introduction   1
   A Look in the Mirror, and a Look Ahead

2. What Is Competitiveness?   21

3. The Industrial Commons   45
   What It Is and Why It Matters

4. When Is Manufacturing Critical to Innovation?   61

5. The Rise and Decline of the American
   Industrial Commons   73

6. Rebuilding the Commons   101
   The Visible Hand of Management

7. Toward a National Economic Strategy
   for Manufacturing   119

   Epilogue   135
   We Can't Turn Back the Clock

Acknowledgments   139
Appendix: Key Component Suppliers for Photovoltaic Unit (India) 141
Notes   145
Index   155
About the Authors   165

Prologue:
Does America Need Manufacturing?

In 1950, manufacturing represented 27 percent of US gross domestic product (GDP) and employed 31 percent of the American workforce. By 2010, manufacturing was only 12 percent of GDP and employed 9 percent of the workforce.[1] Should this trend worry Americans? That is the focal question of this book.

The question "Does manufacturing matter?" is not a new one. In the 1980s, books such as *Restoring Our Competitive Edge* (by our Harvard colleagues Robert Hayes and Steven Wheelwright) and *Manufacturing Matters* (by Berkeley's John Zysman and Stephen Cohen) argued that allowing manufacturing capabilities to erode would be hazardous to a country's economic health. With the Internet boom of the 1990s and Japan's stumbles, however, the issue of manufacturing appeared quaint. The United States was demonstrating its prowess in R&D, software, and services. The Internet spawned a host of new businesses. Electronics companies were prospering by focusing on R&D and outsourcing production to Asian suppliers. Many economists hailed the arrival of "the post-industrial society"[2] and declared that the continued erosion of manufacturing was not just harmless, it was a healthy symptom of economic development: following the same path that agriculture had taken a century before, the shrinking manufacturing sector was now "liberating" resources so that they could be put to high-value-added uses in other sectors, such as services.

We have chosen to revisit this issue at this time for two reasons. First, the "good times" of the 1990s and 2000s were not as good as they first appeared. Average wages for Americans were stagnating, and trade deficits were piling up. Also, after surging in the 1990s, productivity growth slowed down in the 2000s. Meanwhile, in a broad swath of high-technology industries, the center of gravity for both manufacturing and innovation was moving to Asia. And this was all before the Great Recession of 2008! It struck us that the United States had been running a pretty high-stakes experiment: for decades, America has been betting that the erosion of its manufacturing base posed no harm to its long-term economic prospects. Given the stakes, we thought an examination of this assumption and a careful analysis of the data seemed worthwhile.

Our second reason for writing this book was to clarify what we thought were several distortions on both sides of the debate about the importance (or lack of importance) of manufacturing for an economy like America's. On one side of the debate, there has been a misconception about the impact of manufacturing on jobs. "Saving manufacturing" is often equated with saving jobs. With fewer than one in ten members of the American workforce employed in manufacturing, though, it is hard to make the case that manufacturing can be a big job generator—especially because productivity increases due to advances in technology and work processes are a major reason the number of manufacturing jobs in the United States has plunged. In other words, if we expect productivity to continue to increase (which would be a good thing), it gets harder to imagine how even a fairly large surge in manufacturing output would put much of a dent in the American employment picture. We do not deny that there may be a serious employment issue in America.

The fact that manufacturing is unlikely to drive significant job creation, though, often leads too quickly to the conclusion that it is therefore irrelevant. The fallacy in this thinking is quickly revealed by the following statistic: although manufacturing accounts for only

9 percent of the American workforce, the 1.5 million R&D workers employed by US companies in America account for less than 1 percent of the workforce.[3] Yet, no one would suggest that R&D is unimportant to the health of the economy.

This leads us to the second misconception about manufacturing: it is a low-value-added commodity activity that requires low-skill workers and can be easily sourced from anywhere in the world. Unlike R&D, venture capital, or universities, manufacturing is viewed as outside the ecosystem of innovation. It is not "knowledge work," to use the fashionable term. The assumption is that you can lose manufacturing as long as you have innovation. If you believe this portrait, then manufacturing is passé for an innovation-driven economy such as America's.

This perspective, though, just does not square with our observations about what actually happens inside many manufacturing operations. In the course of our careers, we have visited hundreds of factories in just about every industry you can imagine and in just about every corner of the globe. The notion that manufacturing is some low-value-added, low-skill activity that is unconnected to innovation is increasingly a myth. Factories producing sophisticated goods such as biotechnology drugs, flat-panel displays, aircraft engines, semiconductors, specialty materials, and medical devices require very skilled workers who can operate highly complex pieces of precision equipment. In most factories we have visited, we have seen a lot more brain than brawn at work. Manufacturing has become knowledge work.

In addition, manufacturing has connections to the innovation process that often go completely unrecognized. One of us (Gary) spent much of his academic career conducting research on how products in technology-intensive contexts (e.g., biotechnology, medical devices, scientific instruments, and electronics) move their way from R&D into the market. The other (Willy) spent a good chunk of his professional career actually moving products from

R&D to the market and running complex manufacturing and distribution operations in the United States, Mexico, Ireland, Japan, and China. From our contrasting vantage points, we came to a very similar conclusion: manufacturing is often highly integral to the innovation process, and the common assumption that the United States can prosper as an "innovator" without manufacturing is a dangerous one. Indeed, in some contexts, manufacturing is just as important to the innovation ecosystem as strong universities, outstanding R&D, and vibrant venture capital are. The loss of manufacturing competencies should deeply worry Americans.

The problem with these misconceptions about manufacturing is that they often lead to bad decisions by businesses and bad policies by government. For instance, we have seen companies outsource their manufacturing without considering the potential negative impact on their future ability to innovate. We have seen government policy makers ignore the potential value of investing in basic and applied research that might deepen US manufacturing capabilities that support a broad range of sectors. The combination of bad decisions by businesses and inadequate policies by government, we will argue in this book, is leading to an erosion of what we call America's *industrial commons*—the set of manufacturing and technical capabilities that support innovation across a broad range of industries.

Our goal in writing this book is to educate both business leaders and government policy makers about when and where manufacturing matters to an economy. Our thesis is that for the United States, manufacturing matters when it is integral to the process of innovation, and we will provide some frameworks to help identify when and where this is likely to be the case. We are clear that not all manufacturing is integral to innovation. Thus, ours is not a blanket call to save all manufacturing in the United States. It is a call to build manufacturing capabilities in those areas that provide a critical foundation for future innovation.

We have written this book from an American perspective. It focuses on the decline of the American industrial commons, why that has happened, and what American business leaders and government policy makers need to do to reverse this process. However, questions about manufacturing are by no means limited to America. Competition from rapidly industrializing countries such as China and India is pressuring the manufacturing sectors of just about all advanced industrialized economies. Policy makers in the United Kingdom, France, Italy, Denmark, Japan, and even Germany are pondering what the future role of manufacturing in their countries should be. Surprisingly, even in relatively new manufacturing powerhouses such as Taiwan and Korea, competition from China in electronics manufacturing is causing policy makers to ask "Does manufacturing matter?" Although going into the policy issues facing these countries is well beyond the scope of what we can tackle in this book (as well as the scope of our expertise), we hope that readers from outside the United States will see the analogies to their own situations.

We have organized the book as follows. Chapter 1 lays out the basic themes and argument. This chapter also provides a "look in the mirror" using data on US economic performance over the past few decades. This assessment paints a troubling picture. The decline in the performance of manufacturing industries is not just limited to so-called traditional sectors; it has spread to those technology-intensive sectors always viewed as traditional bastions of US economic strength.

Chapter 2 frames our argument within the broader debate about "competitiveness." Although much discussed, the concept of competitiveness is troublingly vague. What does it mean for the United States to be losing this thing called competitiveness? And why does competitiveness matter for economic prosperity? This chapter examines these questions.

Chapter 3 examines how the fate of one industry may be linked to another. Such linkages are often missed in traditional economic statistics that focus on industries. But underlying every industry are sets of technical and operational capabilities, some of which are shared across firms and even across industries. These shared capabilities form what we call the industrial commons. The commons is embedded in suppliers, customers, partners, skilled workers, and local institutions such as universities. Commons are sources of competitiveness for the industries that draw from the shared capabilities. The concept of industrial commons helps to explain how location can provide some firms an advantage.

Chapter 4 examines the role that manufacturing capabilities play in the commons. In particular, it examines the issue of when manufacturing and R&D must be co-located to facilitate innovation. The chapter provides a framework that identifies very specific conditions that make co-location between R&D and manufacturing desirable. These conditions help identify when manufacturing matters to an innovation-based economy and company.

Chapter 5 uses the conceptual apparatus of the previous chapters to analyze the rise and decline of the American industrial commons. The chapter highlights the contributions that both government and private business have historically played in the creation of the American industrial commons as well as their roles in its decline.

Chapter 6 is the first prescriptive chapter and focuses on the roles business leaders and companies can and should play in rejuvenating the commons. Ours is not an appeal to economic patriotism or corporate social responsibility. We argue that companies should be investing in the local industrial commons because it can be a source of competitive advantage. We identify a number of management practices and approaches that have impeded firms from making strategically valuable investments in the commons.

Chapter 7 is our second prescriptive chapter and focuses on government policy. We call for the US government to develop a coherent national economic strategy for manufacturing. However, we forcefully reject many of the common suggestions for improving manufacturing competitiveness, such as protectionism or targeted support to specific industries. Instead, we argue that an economic strategy for manufacturing should focus on two components: building broad capabilities through basic and applied scientific research and investing in the specialized human capital required for today's manufacturing.

PRODUCING PROSPERITY

CHAPTER 1

Introduction

A Look in the Mirror, and a Look Ahead

The financial crisis of 2008 and the ensuing Great Recession was the economic equivalent of a heart attack for the United States. It was not completely unexpected, but struck quickly. It created fear and uncertainty. Once it became apparent we would survive, attention quickly turned to how to nurse the patient back to health and how to prevent another economic heart attack. Much has been written, debated, and discussed about the reforms and regulatory changes that might be needed to prevent another financial meltdown, the right government policies (and particularly fiscal budgetary policies) to jump-start growth and reduce unemployment. There is, however, a big difference between preventing another heart attack and getting the economy on its feet, and becoming fit enough to compete at a world-class level. Lost in the froth of debate over the causes and consequences of the Great Recession of 2008 to 2010 is the fact that the United States has been losing its competitive advantage in those sectors and technologies that it needs to drive growth in the twenty-first century.

For decades, Americans were comforted by the party line that although other countries were becoming much more competitive, our ace in the hole was our ability to innovate and dominate the most advanced industrial sectors. Sure, emerging countries such as China and India might capture the allegedly low-value-added, low-wage sectors, but that was fine; in fact, that was healthy, we were told. American prosperity was ensured by our dominance of the sectors requiring the most advanced technical know-how, such as semiconductors, computers, complex equipment, and aircraft. And the conventional wisdom in the United States was that our more flexible, entrepreneur-centric economic system would ensure that we would stay ahead of the pack and dominate the innovative sectors of tomorrow as well.

This characterization no longer represents reality. Other countries now hold the lead in products such as flat-panel displays, advanced batteries, machine tools, metal forming (castings, stampings, and cold forgings), precision bearings, optoelectronics, solar energy, and wind turbines. Furthermore, US dominance of biotechnology, aerospace, high-end medical devices, and other advanced sectors is under threat.

A combination of company strategies, management thinking, and government policy has led to the gradual erosion of the country's *industrial commons*: the R&D and manufacturing infrastructure, know-how, process-development skills, and engineering capabilities embedded in firms, universities, and other organizations that provide the foundation for growth and innovation in a wide range of industries.[1]

This erosion is the result of a grand economic experiment based on the hypothesis that an advanced economy can continue to prosper and grow even as manufacturing declines because services and other knowledge-based sectors will fill the gap and leave it better off. The stakes involved are enormous. This kind of de-industrialization process can play out over decades. If, in the end, the "manufacturing does not matter" hypothesis proves wrong—and we think that's exactly what's going to happen—the United States (and other countries that have been running the same experiment) will have a big problem on its hands.

The purpose of this book is to persuade business and government leaders to abandon the grand experiment in de-industrialization before it's too late. We argue and present evidence that an industrial commons matters for an advanced economy, explore the underlying causes of its erosion in the United States, and offer ideas about what's needed to reverse that decline.

A Look in the Mirror

The hypothesis that the United States has a competitiveness problem may strike some as odd. Competitiveness was an issue of the 1980s, when policy makers, executives, and academics stood in awe of Japanese companies such as Hitachi, Sony, and Toyota.[2] By the mid-1990s, as the Japanese economy was sagging into a recession that now spans almost two decades, and the US economy—fueled by the Internet and information technology (IT) revolution—sprinted ahead, the competitiveness issue seemed about as dated as legwarmers and Jazzercise. The United States was back on top, and Japan was on its knees.

However, a look at the numbers suggests that we may have declared victory prematurely. Let's start with the US trade balance. Admittedly, it is a rough measure of competitiveness because a currency devaluation can improve a trade balance but reduce real wages and living standards—hardly a positive outcome. (Over the past decade, though, the dollar has depreciated against most of the currencies of America's major trading partners.) In addition, trade balances between the US and individual countries (like China) need to be interpreted carefully because of the complex structure of today's global supply chains. That said, the United States has been

FIGURE 1-1

US trade deficit as percentage of gross domestic product

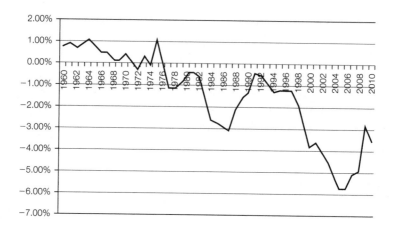

Source: Bureau of Economic Analysis, National Income and Product Accounts table 1.15, last revised January 27, 2012.

running a large and growing total trade deficit (the total value of exports minus imports) since 1960. Figure 1-1 shows the trade deficit's size relative to gross domestic product (GDP) up through 2010.

The huge trade deficit is the reason the United States went from being the world's largest creditor nation in the 1970s to the largest debtor nation. Figure 1-2 depicts the trade performance of the US economy in two basic sectors of the economy: services and manufacturing. This data suggests that the overall US trade deficit is largely a function of the decline of manufacturing competitiveness—or to put it differently, by a significant enough decline that has not been offset by a commensurate rise in service exports.

The inability of the United States to offset its manufacturing trade deficit with a large enough surplus in services is easy to understand once one recognizes that manufactured goods account for about 75 percent of world trade.[3] The relative shares of trade of manufacturing and services have remained relatively constant since

FIGURE 1-2

US trade balance in manufactured goods versus services

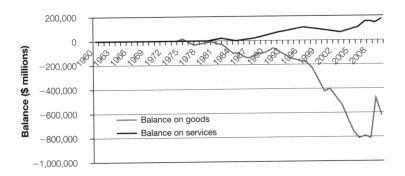

Source: Calculated from Bureau of Economic Analysis data, US International Transactions Accounts table 1, December 15, 2011.

the late 1980s. Services, by their nature, have tended to require local production and, as a result, have been more difficult to export. This is starting to change because of digitization. Whether this helps the US trade balance, though, remains to be seen. Although it means America can potentially export more of some services (such as investment banking and consulting), many others currently performed in the United States (e.g., accounting, data processing, and even medical diagnostics and engineering analysis) can be performed at lower cost overseas. Thus the notion that services exports will soar and bail out the United States requires a huge leap of faith.

The decline in US manufacturing competitiveness, of course, is not a new development. For several decades, production of more traditional goods (textiles, shoes, apparel, furniture, etc.) and heavy industrial goods (steel, shipbuilding, commodity chemical production, etc.) has been gravitating away from high-wage, advanced economies to newly industrializing countries. When the decline of these industries caused significant economic dislocation in the United States in the 1970s and 1980s, optimists hailed it as a healthy transition to technology-intensive sectors that would result in a more dynamic economy, higher growth, and higher wages. At least initially, their view seemed to make sense: the United States had historically run a healthy trade surplus in high tech.

However, that view is contradicted by data assembled in the most recent National Science Foundation report, *Science and Engineering Indicators 2012*.[4] Figure 1-3 shows the trade balances for the United States and selected other countries from 1998 to 2010 in a group of sectors defined by the National Science Foundation as technology intensive: computers and office equipment, communications and semiconductors, scientific instruments, pharmaceuticals, and aircraft.

It is sometimes believed that America's competitiveness problem is due solely to Chinese policies designed to promote its exports and discourage imports.[5] Chinese policies may have had a big impact, but figure 1-3 indicates that the problem transcends China; the Asia-8 group of countries also runs a significant trade surplus in high technology.

FIGURE 1-3

Trade balance in high-technology manufacturing sectors, 1998–2010

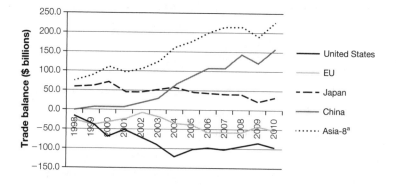

a. Asia-8 includes India, Indonesia, Malaysia, and the Philippines.

Source: Authors' analysis of source data from figure O-37 of National Science Board, *Science and Engineering Indicators 2012* (Arlington, VA: National Science Foundation, 2012).

Additional insight on America's position in high technology can be gleaned by comparing data on the composition of its exports over time with those of other countries. After all, if the United States is a technology powerhouse, we would expect its exports of technology-intensive products as a percentage of its total exports to be relatively high. Figure 1-4 shows World Bank data on high-technology manufactured exports as the percentage of total exports for a selected set of countries in 1992 and 2009.[6]

If we go back to 1992 (the first year that consistent data is available across all the countries examined), we see that high tech accounted for 33 percent of US exports, the highest proportion of any country. The next closest were Japan and the United Kingdom at 24 percent. High tech represented just 6 percent of China's exports. By 2009, the picture had changed significantly. US high-tech exports had declined to 23 percent of its total, the same level as the United Kingdom and France. Among advanced economies, France, Germany, and

FIGURE 1-4

High-technology exports as percentage of total exports

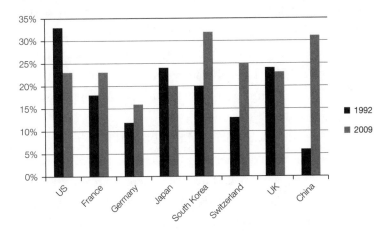

Source: United Nations Commodity Trade Statistics Database; and World Bank, World Development Indicators, http://data.worldbank.org/indicator/TX.VAL.TECH.MF/ZS/country.

Switzerland had increased the technology intensity of their exports. China's high-tech exports had soared to 31 percent of its total, a level surpassed only by South Korea. This data indicates that China has expanded way beyond low-skilled, low-value-added commodities in traditional sectors, and that the world has become a much more competitive place for exactly the kinds of industries that are needed to drive the US economy.

Like all data, this data provides a rearview mirror perspective. It is historical. It does not tell us much about America's ability to compete in growth-generating industries of the future. However, we are already seeing signs that the United States could have trouble competing in critical emerging industries because a significant amount of the needed know-how and infrastructure has already migrated overseas, especially to Asia. Solar power—photovoltaics—is a case in point.

A Look into the Future: The Case of Solar Photovoltaic Cells

Photovoltaic (PV) cells were invented at Bell Labs, and many of the fundamental improvements were developed and commercialized in the United States.[7] American universities, national labs such as the National Renewable Energy Laboratory (NREL), and US companies such as RCA, Boeing, Arco, IBM, and Varian were pioneers in efficient PV designs.

In recent years, the global demand for PV cells has soared. The global installed electricity-generating capacity leapt 152 percent from 2007 to 2008, and an additional 75 percent from 2008 to 2009.[8] Although the first PV devices were invented in the United States, the country is a relatively small manufacturer of PV cells today. According to NREL, 27 percent of global PV production in 2008 was in Europe, 27 percent in China, 18 percent in Japan, 12 percent in Taiwan, and only 6 percent in the United States. The list of the top ten companies in the world in the field included only one US-based company, First Solar, and its manufacturing was split among the United States, Germany, and Malaysia. The rest were predominantly Asian. The NREL *2008 Solar Technologies Market Report* noted that from 1999 to 2004, PV cell and module exports exceeded imports significantly, but this changed in 2005 when exports and imports nearly balanced out. By 2007 imports dominated exports, and by 2009 US Census Bureau trade data showed a $235 million deficit.[9]

Why is the United States behind in the production of PV cells, despite the fact that much of the foundational technology was invented here? One reason is that because PV production draws on many of the same process technologies as microelectronics, Asian companies such as Sharp, Kyocera, and Sanyo were able to leverage their expertise in materials and semiconductors and their proximity to the electronics industry. Asian manufacturers also had an advantage in being proximate to the suppliers of the key components for packaging solar cells into PV modules (the units that go on the roof of your house). The appendix of this book contains a list of suppliers of one Indian company participating in our research. Almost all of the key components had to come from Asia.

The fact that most of the suppliers of key component technologies for solar PV cells and modules are located in Asia should not be surprising. Many of these technologies were shared with other industries—such as semiconductors, flat-panel displays, light-emitting diodes (LEDs) and solid-state lighting, and optical coatings—that had long since moved offshore. Thus, starting a PV factory in the United States requires overcoming a hurdle—the lack of a supplier infrastructure—that is not present in Asia. One way America has tried to overcome this hurdle is through subsidies. Evergreen Solar, for instance, received $58 million in aid from the Commonwealth of Massachusetts to produce PV components in the state.[10] Alas, even with this aid, Evergreen could not produce competitively, and in early 2011 the company announced it was shuttering production in Massachusetts and moving its remaining production to Asia.

The case of solar PV is not an isolated example. Table 1-1 lists some of the capabilities that have vanished or are rapidly vanishing inside the United States—the "endangered species" of the industrial landscape. Like solar PV, all of these technologies had their roots in America. Many were invented inside US universities, often with government funding, or were initially commercialized by American companies. And like solar PV, many of these technologies are critical components of industries with significant growth potential. Rechargeable batteries, for example, are at the heart of more energy-efficient transportation. Machine tools are critical to the defense, aerospace, and automotive industries. LEDs are instrumental to a new generation of energy-efficient lighting.

As discussed at the beginning of this chapter, some economists see no cause for concern. In their eyes, the decline of manufacturing in the United States is a natural and healthy evolution toward a more knowledge-based economy focused on services and innovation.[11] They think it is all right if high-tech products are made in Asia if it means that Americans can buy them at a lower price and can benefit from installing and using them. According to this school, as long as the United States performs the R&D and design, it doesn't really matter economically if manufacturing is performed elsewhere. After all, design is where the value added is, right? Sure, some manufacturing sectors may move to low-wage countries, but other ones—that require greater skills and will pay higher wages— will emerge to take their place.

In this book, we argue that such a perspective is deeply flawed. The data tells a consistent, and alarming, story. When it comes to manufacturing products based on sophisticated technology and

TABLE 1-1

Industrial capabilities that are gone or at risk in the United States: a partial list

Gone or at risk	What happened?
Ultra-heavy forgings	Pressure forging is a way to make high-strength large structures, such as for nuclear reactors or steam generators. The outer vessel of a reactor can weigh over 500 tons and is typically made of seven very large forgings. The Areva Generation III Evolutionary Power Reactor uses four steam generators that weigh 500 tons each. This means the steel mill needs to produce ingots that are 500 to 600 tons each. US mills stopped producing these very large ingots, and US industry gave up on large forgings forty years ago. Only Japan, Korea, China, France, and Russia produce these today.[a]
Machine tools: metal cutting	There was a 43 percent decline in overall metalworking machine shipments from 1990 to 2009, a 40 percent decline in metal cutting, a 62 percent decline in grinding and polishing machines, a 43 percent decline in lathes, a 77 percent decline in station type machines, and a 51 percent decline in the overall metal forming category, which includes punching and shearing machines, bending and forming machines, presses, forging machines, and other metal forming machines.
Permanent magnet electric motors and generators (electric drives)	The leading edge in innovation is neodymium-iron-boron (NeFeB) magnets for use in compact high-performance traction motors and permanent magnet generators. Of the ten to twelve suppliers of permanent magnets, eight to ten are in China, none in the United States.[b]
Rare-earth elements: purification and fabrication of devices using rare-earth elements	The refining of rare-earth elements left the United States with the shutdown of Molycorp's Mountain Pass mine and the relocation of production to China. The downstream effects are the perfect illustration of the destruction of a commons. This is directly tied to the previous item—permanent magnets—but broader.[c]
Rechargeable batteries	The market is dominated mainly by South Korean, Japanese, and Chinese manufacturers. The main reason behind this is their expertise in consumer solutions for lithium ion batteries.

(continued)

TABLE 1-1 (*continued*)

Industrial capabilities that are gone or at risk in the United States: a partial list

Gone or at risk	What happened?
	The Asian Pacific region is a manufacturing hub for all electronic components and has all the supporting infrastructure required for large-scale production of batteries for hybrid electric vehicles (HEVs) and plug-in HEVs.
	North America and the European Union face fierce competition for their lithium ion phosphates from the Asian Pacific manufacturers offering lithium ion manganese chemistries. Those companies pushing for investments in advanced materials, such as nanofabric electrodes and nonmaterial structures, strengthen their expertise in lithium ion batteries.
LED manufacturing for display and energy-efficient lighting	Of the top ten worldwide producers of LEDs in the first quarter of 2010, only one was in the United States—Cree, ranked fifth with a 6.7 percent global market share. Growth in China, Taiwan, and Korea was accelerating. Chinese companies such as LDK Solar were expanding into the production of sapphire substrates, which are the standard material on which blue and white gallium nitride (GaN) LEDs are produced.
Semiconductor manufacturing (foundry services)	Seventy percent of the world's semiconductor foundry capacity is in Taiwan.
Liquid crystal displays (LCDs)	All of the flat-panel display factories in the world are located in Korea, Taiwan, Japan, and China.
Precision glass	Precision glass manufacture is dominated by Japan, with a rapidly emerging capability in China. Some capabilities still exist in Germany.
Fiber optics components, including gallium arsenide (GaAs) laser diodes	As a key part of the electronics supply chain for communications devices, most of the manufacturing of these critical components has been localized to China.

a. Joel S. Yudken, "Manufacturing Insecurity: America's Manufacturing Crisis and the Erosion of the U.S. Defense Industrial Base," report prepared for the Industrial Union Council, AFL-CIO, September 2010, http://www.highroadstrategies.com/downloads/DefIndustrial-Base-Report-FIN.pdf.
b. Gordon Graff, "Remaking the Magnet; Supermagnets: More Pull, Less Weight," *New York Times*, March 30, 1986; James Areddy, "Rare Earths Stay Hot," *Wall Street Journal*, March 23, 2011; and Joel S. Yudken, "Manufacturing Insecurity."
c. "Beijing Cuts Rare-Earth Quotas," *Wall Street Journal*, December 29, 2010.

with significant growth potential, the US competitive position in the world is weakening. The huge current trade deficits are one sign. Even more worrisome, these trends are symptoms of a deeper malaise that has potentially dire consequences. The technical and operational capabilities to manufacture complex products and systems are tightly intertwined with a nation's capacity to generate and capture value from innovations. Manufacturing and innovation share the same industrial commons.

The Erosion of the Industrial Commons

In times past, farmers and local townspeople would bring their livestock to the commons—a local pasture that everyone could use. The commons was a critical community resource because it nourished the livestock that provided a foundation for the local agricultural economy. If the commons fell into disrepair—either through overuse or neglect—everyone suffered. Although taking care of the commons was no individual's responsibility, it was in everyone's interest to do so because all benefited from a healthy commons.[12]

Modern industries have commons as well, although they are infinitely more complex than the simple town greens of centuries past. Today's industrial commons consist of webs of technological knowhow, operational capabilities, and specialized skills that are embedded in the workforce, competitors, suppliers, customers, cooperative R&D ventures, and universities and often support multiple industrial sectors. Although industrial commons are largely supported by private for-profit entities, the knowledge produced by these entities flows across businesses through movements of people from one company to another, supplier–customer collaborations, formal and informal technology sharing, and outright imitation of competitors.

Although there is much talk these days about the world being "flat," in fact, know-how and capabilities are often highly local.[13]

This means that industrial commons can have a local character as well. As a result, companies located in some places have advantages over others by virtue of their access to the appropriate set of workers, engineers, managerial talent, suppliers, and universities. The solar PV industry discussed earlier is an example. Throughout this book, we will document how the presence of an industrial commons can exert a powerful gravitational pull on the location of industries and innovation (and conversely, how the absence of an appropriate commons creates a chasm).

The rough and tumble of international competition means we should expect industries to come and go. Even if this is sometimes painful, it is, in fact, a healthy process by which resources flow to their most productive uses. When a commons erodes, however, it represents a deeper and more systematic problem. It means the foundation upon which future innovative sectors can be built is crumbling. When the semiconductor production business moved to Asia in the 1980s, it brought with it a whole host of capabilities—electronic-materials processing, deposition and coating, and sophisticated test and assembly capabilities—that formed an industrial commons needed to produce a whole host of advanced, high-valued-added electronic products such as flat-panel displays, solid-state lighting, and solar PV.

In this book, we will examine the dynamics that underlie both the rise and decline of commons, and the consequence of those declines. Our argument is built around three core themes.

Theme 1: When a Country Loses the Capability to Manufacture, It Loses the Ability to Innovate

Innovation and manufacturing are often viewed as residing at the opposite ends of the economic spectrum—innovation being all about the brain (knowledge work) and manufacturing all about brawn (physical work). Innovation requires highly skilled, highly paid workers, and manufacturing requires low-skilled, low-paid workers; innovation is a high-valued-added specialty, and manufacturing is a low-value-added commodity; innovation is creative and clean, and manufacturing is dull and dirty.

Such a view of manufacturing is a myth and is based on a profound misunderstanding of how the process of innovation works and the link between R&D and manufacturing. R&D is a critical part of the innovation process, but it is not the whole thing. Innovation is about moving the idea from concept to the customer's hands. For some highly complex products (flat-panel displays, PV cells, and biotechnology drugs, to name a few) the transfer from R&D into production is a messy affair, requiring extremely tight coordination and the transfer of learning between those who design and those who manufacture. If you do not understand the production environment, you have a harder time designing the product. In these settings, there are strong reasons to co-locate R&D and production. It is a lot easier for an engineer to walk across the street to the plant or drive down the road than to fly halfway around the world to troubleshoot a problem. This helps to explain why the American company Applied Materials, a leading maker of equipment for manufacturing semiconductors and solar panels, moved its chief technical officer from the United States to China.[14] Because most of its large customers are now in China, Taiwan, and South Korea, it makes sense for the company to do its research close to the factories that use its equipment. Applied Materials is now moving much of its manufacturing operations to Asia as well. In chapter 4, we will offer a framework for determining when it matters whether R&D and manufacturing are located near each and when it does not.

Theme 2: The Industrial Commons Is a Platform for Growth

The industrial commons perspective suggests that a decline of competitiveness of firms in one sector can have implications for the competitiveness of firms in another. Industries and the suppliers of capabilities to the industries need each other. Kill a critical industry, and the suppliers probably will not survive for long; other industries in the region that depend on those suppliers will then be jeopardized. When the auto industry declines, it causes an atrophy of capabilities (such as casting and precision machining) that are also used in industries such as heavy equipment, scientific instruments, and advanced materials.

The unraveling of a commons is a vicious circle. As capabilities erode, it is harder for companies that require access to stay in business. They are forced to move their operations or their supplier base to the new commons. As they move, it is harder for existing suppliers to sustain themselves. Ultimately, they must either close shop or move their operations.

Even worse, the loss of a commons may cut off future opportunities for the emergence of new innovative sectors if they require close access to the same capabilities. Four decades ago, when US consumer electronics companies decided to move production of these "mature" products to Asia, who would have guessed that this decision would influence where the most important component for tomorrow's electric vehicles—the batteries—would be produced? But that is what happened.[15] The offshoring of consumer electronics production (often contracted to then-little-known Japanese companies such as Sony and Matsushita) led to the migration of R&D in consumer electronics to Japan (and later to South Korea and Taiwan). As consumers demanded ever-smaller, lighter, and more powerful (and power hungry!) mobile computers and cell phones, electronics companies were pushed to innovate in batteries. In the process, Asia became the hub for innovation in the design and manufacturing of compact, high-capacity, rechargeable, lithium ion batteries, a technology that was invented in America. This explains why Asian suppliers have become the dominant source of the lithium ion battery cells used in electric vehicles.

Theme 3: There Is Nothing "Natural" About Erosion of the Industrial Commons — Management and Policy Matter

The erosion of the industrial commons in the United States is the result not of the "invisible hand" of markets but rather the "visible hand" of managers and policy makers. The skills, know-how, and capabilities underpinning an industrial commons accumulate over time. Both government policies and the investment decisions of private enterprises determine what capabilities are fostered where. Decisions by US companies to outsource a growing array of increasingly complex processes (including product R&D) and to reallocate resources away from long-term research have played a central role in the erosion of the US industrial commons.

As we shall discuss, each of these individual decisions, when viewed in isolation, may look like it makes perfect sense. Cumulatively and collectively, however, they have serious consequences for both a country and individual companies.

Consider outsourcing. For many companies, it was simply far too attractive to shutter their production in the United States and have Asian suppliers make the products. Many companies have even decided to buy their R&D from suppliers in Asia as well. (For instance, most laptop computers are designed and manufactured by a small handful of Taiwanese companies.) In the short term, such outsourcing could dramatically lower the costs of goods and supercharge earnings, which is tough logic to combat. Yet, as each company makes such a decision, it becomes increasingly difficult for existing suppliers to stay in business. Investing in new technologies or training workers becomes less economically feasible. This lack of investment in technological and human resources leads to further erosion in competitive performance, which makes it even more attractive for other companies to move their supply base overseas. The process looks like a natural reaction to market forces, but, in fact, it was driven by some very specific management decisions.

Government policy, too, plays a huge role, even in highly market-oriented economies like America's. There was nothing natural about the creation of the United States' strength in science-based industries. Government policy played a critical role. After World War II, the US government began to implement a policy of massive support for basic scientific research through newly created agencies such as the National Science Foundation (NSF) and the National Institutes of Health (NIH), and through existing agencies such as the Department of Defense and Department of Energy.[16] Cumulatively, these investments established the basic sciences that laid the institutional foundations for innovations in semiconductors, high-speed computers, computer graphics, broadband communications, mobile telephony, the Internet, and modern genomics-based methods of drug discovery. Reversing the decline of the US industrial commons will require both effective management and government policy.

Our Perspective

Competitiveness and our future economic welfare are topics that are passionately debated. Some see the problem as a negative by-product of globalization. Some see free trade as the problem. Some advocate a strong policy with the government playing a leading role in driving industrial development. Some want less government involvement. Some see the problems as government (either by omission or commission), whereas others see the problem as American management. Some see the problem as China (import barriers and currency manipulation), whereas some see the problem as America (a declining educational system and a culture too heavily focused on today's consumption over tomorrow's growth).

We enter these inquiries with our own biases and perspectives, as follows:

- *Free trade is not the problem.* The United States (and every other country) can benefit from a system of relatively free and open trade. US imports from China are not the problem per se. Consider the US trade deficit in high technology with China that emerged in the 1990s. A major chunk of this was in the computers and communications equipment that formed the backbone of the IT revolution in America. Those imports played an extremely important role in driving US productivity growth. Intense competition among suppliers around the world certainly played a role in reducing the cost of this IT equipment. Import barriers or other trade restrictions that increased the prices of imports would have done far more harm than good by choking off investment in productivity-enhancing IT.

  This is not to ignore the legitimate and serious concerns about China's trade policies and the quid pro quo it extracts from foreign companies investing there. But we argue that fighting to open trade (and that includes removing barriers erected by the United States and Europe) should be the goal, not creating additional barriers.

- *Believing in the power of markets does not preclude the judicious use of appropriate government policies.* Markets are a splendid thing. They solve many complex problems far better than any other institutional arrangement. But they do not solve all problems. Debate on competitiveness too often bifurcates into two extreme camps: advocates of strong-armed government policy (with little trust in markets) and proponents of laissez-faire economics who strongly distrust government. The history of the United States shows that market-based solutions and government involvement are not incompatible. In fact, markets and government policies can be highly complementary weapons in economic development.

- *Government can create the right conditions, but ultimately, management decisions will determine what happens.* We will discuss government policies that can help set the stage for renewal of American competitiveness. They are important. Ultimately, however, America's competitiveness problems are not going to be solved solely by government. The problems are rooted in the toolbox of management practices, approaches, and philosophies—many developed and propagated by business schools and consulting firms—that have systematically led American companies to cede advantages in technology-intensive sectors. If production workers are using the wrong technology to perform their jobs, we cannot expect them to be very effective. The same applies to managers.

- *In a global economy, we cannot expect managers to make decisions based solely on national loyalty. Markets matter.* CEOs who make de cisions to set up operations outside their home country or to outsource to overseas suppliers are sometimes tarred as "unpatriotic" or, as Senator John Kerry disparaged them in the 2004 presidential campaign, "Benedict Arnold CEOs."[17] But to which country should CEOs be loyal? The home country of the corporate headquarters? The location of the majority of the company's employees? The location of the majority of its shareholders? The CEO's country of origin? The answer to the question is hardly clear. What is more, we cannot expect today's managers, who operate in a highly competitive market for corporate control and executive talent, to take one for the team. Even if they did, it would likely be unhealthy for an economy. Investing in the industrial commons is not a matter of patriotism; it is a matter of good business leadership.

CHAPTER 2

What Is Competitiveness?

Should business leaders in a country like the United States worry about the competitiveness of the national economy? Should government policy makers be concerned about how competitive their country's or region's economy is relative to others? Since a central purpose of this book is to help business leaders and government policy makers understand how their respective actions affect the competitiveness of the US economy and the health of its industrial commons, we need to provide a clear definition of competitiveness and how the competitiveness of a country differs from that of a company.

We define the competitiveness of a country as *the advantage workers and organizations located in one place—a local commons—enjoy in the production of specific goods or services over workers and organizations located elsewhere.* For workers, this advantage means being able to attract and sustain higher wages through higher productivity. For organizations, this advantage is the differential in cost or quality of products or services produced elsewhere.

Before plunging into an elaboration, let us clarify one thing about our terminology. For shorthand, we use the term *country* or *nation* as our relevant unit of geographic analysis. In a discussion of competitiveness, however, country is often only relevant when one is discussing national policies and conditions (e.g., exchange rates) that might influence competitiveness. In a country as large as the United States, different *regions* (New England, the Midwest, etc.) and states may have very different competitive capabilities, and people with the requisite skills to produce a particular product (e.g., automobiles) may be found in various states and compete with each other for jobs. Sometimes the relevant region may span national boundaries—for example, the design of sophisticated machine tools is concentrated in a commons that includes parts of Switzerland, Italy, and Germany. However, since saying "region or country or both" every time we discuss competitiveness would be cumbersome, we will simply use the term *country*.

The Competitiveness of Countries and Companies

Competition takes place at two levels. The most visible are the product markets in which enterprises compete. At this level, what matters is how, say, German automobile companies do against American automobile companies in the market for cars. When a country can produce better cars (at the same price) or can produce cars more efficiently, it has an advantage.

A second, less-visible layer at which national competition occurs is in what economists call "the factor input markets" that provide labor, capital, and other resources needed to operate. For the purposes of understanding social prosperity, the most important market is the labor market where people—front-line operators, supervisors, midlevel managers, engineers, scientists, executives, and so forth—compete every day for jobs. Groups of software engineers living in

Silicon Valley and Bangalore vie for opportunities. The same is true of assembly-line workers at plants in Michigan, Mexico, Brazil, Mississippi, and Japan, and drug-discovery chemists in Basel, New Jersey, Boston, and San Diego. *A country's living standards improve when the people who live there outcompete others in the labor market.* Thus if we care about prosperity and standards of living, we need a definition of competitiveness that explicitly takes into account the economic rewards to human capital.

There is clearly a tight connection between the competitiveness of enterprises and the competitiveness of workers in the same country. If workers do not have appropriate skills for a certain type of job, then local enterprises requiring those skills will clearly be at a disadvantage against firms from elsewhere with access to appropriately skilled personnel. They will either be forced to move their operations or will be unable to compete in product markets against those firms from countries with workers possessing the requisite skills. But if enterprises are not competitive because they are poorly managed, have bad technology, or lack other complementary assets (e.g., a local distribution channel), then even highly skilled workers will be at a disadvantage. Labor productivity is partly a function of a worker's endowed skill (education and training) and partly a function of the worker's access to capital and technology.

The competitiveness of a company and a country also differ. Most standard definitions talk about the competitiveness of a country as a nation's ability to sell goods and services on open, international markets. From this perspective, the competitiveness of a company and a country would appear to be similar. But there are two fundamental distinctions:

1. *Unlike competitions between businesses (and sports teams), international trade is not a zero-sum game.* Corporate competitions, like most sports competitions, have winners and losers.

When IBM gains market share at the expense of Hewlett-Packard in the server market, there is no silver lining for HP; it has lost, and IBM has won. In contrast, exports of German-made machine tools to China benefit Germans; increase the productivity of companies that manufacture wind turbines in China, which benefits the Chinese; and can lower the cost of building wind farms in Vietnam, a country considered ideal for leveraging wind power. This is the basis of comparative advantage trade theory, which was first articulated by British economist David Ricardo in the early nineteenth century. Of course, not all companies in these countries would be winners. German machine-tool companies compete with each other for that business in China, and some might do better than others. The same is true of the Chinese wind-turbine producers. Some companies win, and some lose.

2. *A company's employees are more or less organized around the goal of advancing the company's position in the market, but, at the country or regional level, uniformity of purpose breaks down.* Organizations and workers *within* countries or regions compete as vigorously against each other as they do against foreign rivals. The biotech industry in the greater Boston–Cambridge area is composed of hundreds of competing firms; they are not on the same team. Biogen Idec at one end of Kendall Square and Sanofi's Genzyme unit at the other both sell drugs for multiple sclerosis, and neither one has any interest in helping the other do better. An electronics assembly plant in the Guangdong province of China worries just as much about its competitor across the street as it does about factories in Japan, Korea, Taiwan, Mexico, eastern Europe, and elsewhere.

A Country's Advantage

A country has an advantage in a particular activity when it can attract capital, organizations that supply jobs and complementary know-how, and other resources needed for its workforce to productively engage in the creation of goods and services.

There are two telltale tests of competitiveness. First, the organizations operating in that country are doing well by standard measures: their products are meeting the test of competition against producers from elsewhere in terms of market share, profitability, and so on. Second, workers are benefiting from increases in real wages (adjusted for purchasing power). Note that this criterion excludes "competitiveness" that results from devaluation of a currency (which suppresses real wages) or from other methods of suppressing wages.

Our definition of a country's competitiveness is similar in some ways and different in others from those of other economists. Like Michael Porter of Harvard and Paul Krugman of Princeton, we see productivity as being at the heart of competitive advantage.[1] High labor productivity makes it possible to provide workers with high wages without creating a disadvantage in unit-labor costs. Our definition is also consistent with that of Laura D'Andrea Tyson of the University of California, Berkeley, who defines a country's competitiveness as its ability to "produce goods and services that meet the test of international competition while its citizens enjoy a rising and sustainable standard of living."[2] The latter part of this definition—a rising and sustainable standard of living—is related to wages that are driven by productivity.[3]

Our definition differs from theirs in the emphasis it places on human capital. In our model of competition, it is not just firms that are competing to sell products in international and domestic markets; workers are also competing to sell their labor. As we discuss in the following section, this focus on human capital in the competitiveness equation is particularly germane in an increasingly globalized world, where capital and factors of production other than labor tend to be relatively mobile.

Human Capital and Competitiveness

To understand why competitiveness matters at a national level, one needs to understand a concept in economics known as *factor mobility*. Factors of production include things such as land, natural resources, financial resources, physical capital (e.g., equipment), and, of course, human capital. Factor mobility refers to the extent to which a particular factor of production (say, workers) can move geographically. Mobility matters because the more mobile a factor is, the more flexible it can be in eluding competition—you just go where the competition is not. Mobility is a great advantage. Alas, not every factor of production is equally blessed with mobility.

At one extreme, land and natural resources tend to be extremely immobile. This means that if it becomes much more costly to extract coal in West Virginia than Brazil (as a result of, say, regulation, taxes, lack of technology, or relatively higher wage costs), the owner of the former mine has a big problem and there is not a lot it can do about it.

At the other end of the mobility spectrum, financial capital can be moved around the globe very quickly and at very little cost. With a few clicks of a mouse, $100 in an American company's stock can be converted to 76 euros' worth of stock in a European company. If General Electric decides to invest more to grow its operations in, say, India, it can easily move the required capital to its Indian operations. Such mobility is a great advantage because it allows investors (individual, institutional, and multinational) to redeploy resources to the location they think offers the best return.

Organizations have varying degrees of mobility, depending on their size. A small retailer in your local town is probably not very mobile, whereas multinational corporations are quite mobile. They routinely open new operations (e.g., factories, R&D centers) in far-flung corners of the globe and close others. In 2010, US multinationals invested approximately $330 billion outside the United States (including both new equity investments and retained earnings) and collectively owned close to $4 trillion in assets outside the United States.[4] Such mobility is a great advantage. If a particular country becomes a more attractive place for production as a result of changes in costs, regulations, or taxes, a firm that can move its production to that location has a great advantage over the one that is stuck somewhere less desirable.

Human capital tends to have very limited mobility. Certainly, people relocate to get new jobs. (The authors of this book have moved several times during their careers.) Most people, however, consider frequent moves (e.g., every one, two, or three years) to be intolerably disruptive. Moreover, most of us have some geographic limits to where we will move. Cultural and language barriers (let alone immigration restrictions) constrain our choices.

Consider this: Americans have a reputation for being relatively mobile. However, according to Census Bureau data, in 2008–2009, only 2.3 percent of the employed population between the ages of twenty-four and sixty-five relocated across state boundaries. The vast majority (90 percent) did not move at all, and most moves occurred within the same county (7.5 percent).[5] Compared with the European Union (EU), where about between 0.1 percent and 0.3 percent of the working-age population moves across country borders in any given year, this is a relatively high level of mobility.[6] Still, it's not as if Americans are jumping from state to state. Furthermore, the percentage of Americans moving outside the United States is a miniscule 0.3 percent (right about the EU level for cross-border moves).

Workers' limited mobility means they are highly vulnerable to shifts in competitive advantage. If you are a highly skilled semiconductor designer in the San Francisco Bay area and it becomes a much less attractive place for semiconductor companies to source design work, you might be faced with the choice of moving or finding another line of work. Those with specialized skills (such as machinists) who worked for the auto industry in the Detroit area felt this keenly as auto companies moved production away from their region. Some relocated, but some could not. Those who could not often had to change occupations. Thus, the competitiveness of a place matters most to the people who work and live there because, unlike investors, they cannot rapidly redeploy their (human) capital anywhere on earth.

This is why changes in the competitiveness of countries or regions can have significant effects on prosperity. When the Santa Clara Valley became an attractive place for entrepreneurs to establish semiconductor and computer companies (and later software and Internet companies), a quiet agricultural economy based on walnuts and apricots became one of the most vibrant and prosperous places in the world. India's growing attractiveness as a place to carry out software engineering has spawned a growing middle class of engineers and managers. Conversely, as Michigan and the Upper Midwest became a relatively less attractive place to manufacture automobiles, unemployment soared, real estate prices fell, buildings deteriorated, public services eroded, and life became terribly difficult for many people.

A More Competitive World

In a business school class, a standard exercise is assessing the level of competition facing a company, the threat of entry of other enterprises that make the same or substitute products, and the degree to which that company sells into markets in which buyers hold a relatively strong bargaining position.[7] Such an analysis of competitive forces can also be very useful for understanding the long-term wage prospects of a workforce. A fundamental principle in economics is that competition leads to erosion of prices and returns. For a company, competition in product markets reduces profits. For a workforce, competition in labor markets reduces wages.

Historically, competition in labor markets was largely local. Workers competed for jobs against workers (with similar skills) from the same region. Competition might increase due to inward migration (for instance, when agricultural workers left farms to seek higher-paying jobs in the cities, or when Americans living on the East Coast headed west to seek new opportunities). After World War II, the scope of competition in the labor market enlarged as some industries migrated from one region of the United States to another. In the 1950s, New England textile workers started to realize that their most serious competition for jobs was not coming from their fellow Red Sox fans but from Americans living in lower-wage southern states. Still, until the 1970s, competition for labor in the United States was largely confined to inside the country's borders.

The picture today is very different. A combination of reduced trade barriers, freer flows of capital, reduced transportation costs, reliable high-speed communication networks, and other forces of globalization has enlarged the geographic scope of labor market competition considerably beyond US borders.

Globalization by itself would have intensified the competition facing the US worker. Now consider the additional supply of global labor created by four populous countries—China, India, Russia, and Brazil—that have joined the world economic system in the past two decades. In 2010, China alone had a workforce of 780 million people; India, 478 million, Brazil, 95 million; and Russia, 75 million.[8] Combined, this represented the addition of 1.4 *billion* people to the global labor force since 1990.[9] Let's put that figure in perspective. In 1990, the US workforce was 125 million; the workforce of its top five trading partners that year (Canada, Japan, Mexico, Germany, and the United Kingdom) was 158 million *combined*.[10] So, very roughly speaking, for every other American worker an American was competing against, he or she was competing against one foreign worker. By 2010, the US labor force had grown to 154 million, but the labor force of America's top five trading partners (which by then included China) had exploded to 951 million (obviously, most of this growth can be attributed to China).[11] By 2010, for every American worker an American was competing with, he or she was competing against six foreign workers. Although we should not take these ratios too literally, they provide a rough picture of how much bigger the global labor pool in which Americans swim has become.

By themselves, these numbers only tell us crudely that the labor pool has expanded globally, but they tell us nothing about competition between workers competing in different segments of the labor market. Clearly, there are different segments of the labor market, and international competition affects those segments differently. First, we need to consider that many sectors of an economy are inherently local (e.g., retail, health care, car repair, home building) and that the risk of a job in those sectors being moved from one country to another is extremely low. A nurse at a Boston-area hospital does not compete against a nurse in a Beijing hospital for a job. Second, we need to consider skills and education. Because of differences, workers in different parts of the world are not perfect substitutes for each other even if they work in the same sectors.

Nonetheless, the degree of expansion of global competition in labor markets is still striking. Consider the expansion of trade. Obviously, the more an economy relies on trade, the more workers from that country are competing directly with workers from other parts of the world. Table 2-1 shows the percentage of GDP

TABLE 2-1

Trade as percentage of gross domestic product: 1981 versus 2008

Country	Merchandise		Services	
	1981	2008	1981	2008
United States	16.5	24	3.3	6.5
Canada	47	58	6.8	10.5
Mexico	21	56	5.4	4.0
Japan	25	31	5.1	6.5
Germany	44	72	9.2	15.2
United Kingdom	40	41	12	18.5
China	22	57	0	6.8
India	12	42	3.2	15.8
Brazil	18	23	2.8	4.7

Source: Data from World Bank, World Development Indicators, http://data.worldbank.org/
indicator/TG.VAL.TOTL.GD.ZS.

accounted for by total trade (imports plus exports). Not surprisingly, trade has become a much more important component in the economic life of countries. At 24 percent, the United States had a relatively low trade-to-GDP ratio in 2008, but this was a result of the much larger size of the US economy. And at 24 percent, the impact of trade on US economic performance is not trivial (although, as has been pointed out by Paul Krugman, this data shows that a lot of improvement in economic welfare depends on what you do in nontrade sectors).[12] Even in services, where trade is much smaller, there is a sharp upward trend.

The upward trend (in both merchandise and services) supports the idea that workers from all countries, not just the United States, are increasingly competing in a more globalized market for labor. The increased exposure to trade is not at all a bad thing in and of itself. Competition cuts both ways: it is a threat but also an opportunity.

To get a better sense of what increased trade means to patterns of competition in labor markets, let's look at recent work by Michael Spence and Sandile Hlatshwayo of New York University, who examined structural changes in the US economy, employment trends, and trade.[13] They divided US industries into two categories: "tradable" and "nontradable" sectors.

Tradable sectors comprise those goods and services that can be produced in one country and consumed in another country. Tradable sectors include most manufactured products, energy, raw materials, agricultural products, and services such as tourism, higher education, business and technical consulting, commercial banking, data processing, communications, and digital media.

Spence and Hlatshwayo define nontradable sectors as those requiring production and consumption to occur in the same country. Nontradable sectors include things such as government, health care, retail, construction, restaurants, hotels, most legal services, most real estate, and any other service requiring local delivery (e.g., haircuts, car maintenance). The distinction between tradable and nontradable is not always sharp, and the boundary has certainly shifted in the past few decades as a result of technical changes (and particularly IT) that make it increasingly efficient to deliver certain services remotely.

By dividing industries into internationally tradable and nontradable sectors, Spence and Hlatshwayo provide a nice way to test how well US workers are competing in the international markets for labor. What they find is both striking and disturbing. Between 1990 and 2008, 97.7 percent of employment growth in the United States took place in the nontradable sectors (and of this, 40 percent was due to government and health care). In the internationally tradable sectors, employment growth was essentially flat, and only in high-end services such as management and consulting services, banking, computer systems design, and insurance was there growth. This growth, however, was completely offset by job losses in the manufacturing sector. Most of these jobs were in lower-value-added parts of the value chain. But, as the authors point out:

> *[A]s the emerging markets grow, they will compete for more sophisticated functions. This does not mean that the United States will lose all the sectors in which it has developed a comparative advantage—just that more potential competition is on the horizon.*[14]

When we consider the previously discussed analyses of the total growth in the worldwide labor pool, the growth in trade, and the employment trends in tradable sectors of the US economy, it becomes easy to understand the root causes of the well-documented stagnation in average real wages in the United States since 1980. The typical US worker today is facing far greater competition for his or her services, and this competition is exerting predictable downward pressure on wages.

Let's now turn to the issue of skill levels. Skills are a logical way to segment labor markets. Lawyers tend to compete with lawyers, mechanical engineers with mechanical engineers, and university graduates with other university graduates. The degree to which US workers are exposed to foreign competition depends partly on whether they have differentiated skills. Several studies, including the Spence and Hlatshwayo paper just discussed, have found that workers at the lower end of the skill/educational spectrum have been the most negatively affected by competition from foreign workers. Although the vast majority of the labor force in emerging economies such as China, India, or Brazil (the places adding the most to the global labor pool) may exhibit a skill deficit relative to US workers, that doesn't mean that US workers have no cause to worry.

In 2000 (the most recent year for which comparable data were available) about 25 percent of all people with at least some tertiary

education (ranging from completion of a post–high school technical program to a doctorate) lived in the United States. That was the
highest proportion in the world. But the next three largest percent-
ages were found in China, India, and Russia.[15]

A study by the National Science Foundation of the number of
university graduates with degrees in science and engineering in a set
of countries in 2004 shows that the increasing level of competition
in the global labor market is not just limited to the low end of the
skills spectrum (table 2-2).

Clearly, data such as this has limits. It is difficult to compare the
quality and content of programs across countries—the number of

TABLE 2-2

University degree (first) by country in science and engineering, 2004

Country	Science and engineering graduates (total)	Engineering graduates
United States	455,848	64,675
European Union (total)	617,469	212,267
Germany	108,730	27,662
United Kingdom	109,940	19,780
Japan (2005)	349,015	97,931
Taiwan	85,891	46,870
India (1990)	176,036	29,000
China	672,463	442,463
Brazil (2002)	92,040	28,024
Russia (2006)	293,729	131,688

Source: National Science Board, Science and Engineering Indicators 2008, vol. 2 (Arlington, VA: National Science Foundation), A2-102–A2-104.

years of study, for instance, varies, and an engineering graduate from a small university in China is unlikely to be as qualified as an MIT-trained engineer. That said, it's clear that China, India, Brazil, and Russia are not only contributing low-skilled labor to the world labor pool but that scientists and engineers in the United States and Europe are already and will increasingly find themselves competing with engineers from India, China, Russia, and Brazil.

The fact that India and eastern Europe have become major outsourcing hubs in software and IT support for American and European companies tells us something about the quality of their technical workforces. So do global patterns of R&D spending. China is currently the third-largest spender on R&D (after the United States and Japan).[16] Since 2000, R&D spending in China has been increasing at an average annual rate of 19 percent (compared with 3.3 percent in the United States and 3.3 percent in the European Union).[17] Brazil and India now rank among the top fifteen R&D-spending countries in the world.

The growing attractiveness of China, India, and other emerging countries as locations for higher-value-added activities such as R&D is also evident in Bureau of Economic Analysis data on R&D spending by US multinationals. According to that data, US multinationals have increased the share of their R&D spending occurring in foreign subsidiaries from 9 percent in 1989 to 15.6 percent in 2009.[18] This data understates the amount of R&D that US-based multinationals are sourcing from these countries. When firms buy design or technical services from a third-party outsourcer, the expense is typically reported as part of their cost of goods sold, not R&D; therefore, it does not appear in the foreign direct investment (FDI) statistics.

Again, our point is not that eastern Europe and countries such as China, India, Brazil, and Russia have achieved parity with the United States in terms of skill levels. They have not—*yet*. But to assume that they lack the human resources to move beyond low-wage, low-value-added activities discarded by the United States and western Europe flies in the face of the facts. Moreover, to assume that these countries will not move up the skills ladder over time flies in the face of everything that the history of economic development—from that of the United States to Japan to South Korea—has taught us.

Implications and Reactions

Data like that presented earlier in this chapter typically provokes one of three reactions, which are explored in this section.

TRY TO TURN BACK THE CLOCK

From one perspective, globalization, by flooding the world labor market with low-wage workers, has and will continue to erode the wages of people living in the United States and other advanced economies. After all, the thinking goes, how can a worker in America earning $30 per hour compete with a Chinese worker making $50 per week? At its extreme, proponents of this view are repulsed by free trade and see the answer to America's (and Europe's) competitive problems to be building a fortress of trade barriers and other protectionist measures. During the 1992 presidential campaign, candidate Ross Perot (who received 19 percent of the popular vote) predicted that if the North American Free Trade Agreement (NAFTA) were passed, there would be dire consequences for American jobs: "a giant sucking sound going south." Perot went on to publish a book whose title, *Save Your Job, Save Our Country: Why NAFTA Must Be Stopped—Now*, pretty much summarizes the anti-free-trade perspective.[19]

Perot has plenty of company. An NBC/*Wall Street Journal* poll conducted in 2010 found that 69 percent of Americans believed that free trade with other countries had cost the United States jobs, and 53 percent believed that free trade had hurt the country overall.[20] Support for free trade in the US Congress also runs shallow. The Senate dragged its feet on ratifying a free-trade agreement with South Korea that was originally signed in June 2007.[21]

The politics behind free trade are complex. Getting the right structure for agreements is by no means trivial, given the political interests of the countries involved. Many who have criticized US policy on free trade—such as Clyde Prestowitz—correctly argue that the *real* international trade system, larded with government subsidies, local-content requirements, forced sharing of intellectual property, currency-rate management, outright protectionism, and other policy manipulations—is far from being the free market of textbook economics.[22]

Nevertheless, it seems to us that reducing these barriers and distortions would be the right direction for policy, not erecting bigger barriers. The integration of countries such as China, India, Brazil, and Russia and other emerging economies into the global system has a number of very big benefits. Clearly, it helps lift millions (and potentially billions) of people out of poverty. The growing middle classes in India and China are testament to this. In eastern Europe, highly educated workers with university degrees in math and computer science are no longer underemployed as construction workers or street cleaners; thanks to trade, they are now finding well-paying jobs in the burgeoning IT-outsourcing sector.

Greater prosperity around the world does not threaten American interests or reduce American prosperity and clearly has geopolitical benefits in terms of stability. Even more important, although every one of those new members of the global workforce creates competition for jobs (everywhere), he or she also creates new sources of demand. Thus, that Indian software engineer who got a job that might have gone to an American or Finnish programmer now has the money to buy American goods and to travel to the United States.

This does not mean there are not winners and losers from trade. Software engineers and production workers who lose *their* jobs are clearly worse off. But building barriers only serves to stifle competition and squash the incentive (at the individual, company, and national levels) to become even more fit to compete. That would be a losing proposition for any country.

If you had to pick just one elixir for economic growth and prosperity, it would be productivity. Productivity drives economic growth and standards of living. Generally, economists focus on two measures of productivity: labor productivity and total factor productivity. Labor productivity—as the name implies—is the amount of output (value) created per hour of labor expended. Wages are *highly* correlated with labor productivity across sectors and countries. Comparison of wages across countries is really meaningless without reference to productivity differences. Total labor costs are a function of wages (labor costs per hour) times productivity (output per hour). High levels of productivity (like we have in the United States) allow workers to receive higher wages without creating a total labor-cost disadvantage. For instance, the US workforce has, on average, a 3:1 productivity advantage over the Mexican workforce. This means that US wages can be three times higher without creating a per-unit-labor-cost disadvantage vis-à-vis Mexican workers.

Total factor productivity (TFP) combines all inputs—labor, capital, and others—to create a measure of overall efficiency for an economy. TFP is driven by innovation in products and processes and is important because it influences the attractiveness of a country for carrying out productive activities. It is, in some ways, a nice summary statistic of competitiveness. It is also probably the single best predictor of the overall long-term prosperity of a country. Part of the reason is that high TFP will give a country an advantage in international markets (e.g., it will be able to produce similar-quality products at lower costs than an economy with low TFP). But high

TFP makes things better even in sectors where there is no international trade. If, for instance, grocery stores in your local area have been increasing their TFP, you will benefit from their enhanced efficiency (e.g., through lower prices) even though they do not engage in any international trade.

If you believe in the primacy of productivity (as we do), then your degree of optimism hinges on how you interpret recent trends in productivity growth and your projections of future productivity growth. To get a better handle on productivity trends and the underlying drivers of productivity growth, we turned to the work of Harvard's Dale Jorgenson.[23] For the past five decades, no one has done more than he to pioneer new methods for measuring productivity and analyzing reams of data across industries, time, and countries to get a clear picture about the contributors to productivity growth. As figure 2-1 shows, he found that the labor productivity performance of the US economy has varied over long time periods.

The United States suffered a significant productivity slowdown from the early 1970s to about the mid-1990s, a period generally

FIGURE 2-1

Labor productivity performance of the US economy

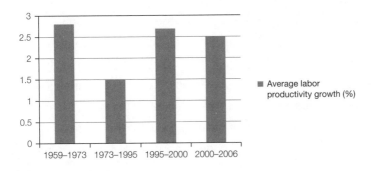

■ Average labor productivity growth (%)

Source: Figure created from data presented in table 1 in Dale W. Jorgenson, Mun S. Ho, and Kevin J. Stiroh, "A Retrospective Look at the US Productivity Growth Resurgence," *Journal of Economic Perspectives* 22, no. 1 (2008): 3–24.

associated with weak economic performance. Then, beginning in the mid-1990s, productivity growth surged. This was not only good performance by historical standards; it also bested just about every other major developed country during the same time period. Detailed statistical analysis by Jorgenson and his colleagues clearly points to information technology as the chief driver of this productivity resurgence. From 1995 to 2000, most of the productivity growth of the US economy came from the sectors that created information technology (e.g., computers, semiconductors, software, and telecommunications equipment). From 2000 to 2006, the chief drivers of productivity growth shifted to the sectors that *used* information technology (e.g., financial services, retail, and manufacturing). As these sectors began to invest heavily in new IT systems (e.g., online customer service and sales, enterprise resource planning software), they experienced their own productivity surges that reverberated through the economy. In many ways, the IT-driven productivity surge of the mid-1990s to the mid-2000s—which combined strong technical advances with flexibility in adopting new technology, new business models, and new operating processes—represents the best of American dynamism. It is certainly cause for optimism.

The question, though, is whether such performance can be sustained. A few facts make us cautious. First, Jorgenson's analysis makes painfully clear how narrow the sources of productivity growth can be. For the period from 1995 to 2000, sectors comprising only 3 percent of the GDP were driving most of the increase in productivity. This clearly refutes the argument often made by economists that some sectors are not more important than others for generating long-term growth. Semiconductor chips turned out to be a lot more important than potato chips for driving productivity growth.[24]

Second, a big driver of labor productivity growth is increases in the ratio of capital to labor (what economists call "capital deepening"). This is what was happening from 1995 to 2000: companies were investing heavily in IT (new computer systems, new software, etc.), which made workers who had been doing tasks manually much more productive (e.g., think about computer-aided design). After 2000, however, increases in capital-to-labor ratios were driven more by decreasing labor hours than by increasing capital investments. As Jorgenson reports, between 2000 and 2006 nonresidential investment grew at an average annual rate of only 1 percent (compared with an average rate of 5.4 percent for the period from 1959 to 2000). Productivity was not being increased by arming workers with more and better capital (thereby allowing them to increase output); it was being accomplished by using fewer workers. Whether you increase productivity by increasing or decreasing the numerator or denominator of productivity (output/labor hours) is mathematically equivalent, but, of course, each has very different implications for economic well-being.

A similar trend of "adding by subtracting" can also be seen in the data on value added per worker in the manufacturing sectors. Value added per worker has generally increased in manufacturing quite dramatically over the past decade. Again, this looks like the triumph of productivity. Upon closer examination, however, much of the increase is actually due to the decline in lower-value-added manufacturing sectors that have moved offshore. That would be great if the resources liberated from those low-value-added sectors were being redeployed to higher-value-added uses, but there is no evidence that this was the case. Manufacturing employment continued to decline even as the value added increased. At the margin, as the next-lowest-value-added sector is eliminated, value added per person will continue to increase. Again, statistically, this *is* a productivity increase, but it is not a productivity increase driven by growth-enhancing innovation in products and processes.

Finally, the most recent trends in productivity and employment are not cause for optimism. Of course, starting with the Great Recession of 2008, it is very hard to sort out shorter-term business-cycle effects from longer-term trends, and the extreme nature of the most recent business cycle only makes the usual challenge even more difficult. But even before 2008, there were signs that productivity was reverting to a more staid pace. Jorgenson's analysis shows that productivity growth rates peaked in 2004 and then reverted to the low levels of the 1970s and 1980s during the 2004 to 2007 period. Although US productivity surged during the Great Recession, almost all of this surge appears to be due to dramatic reductions in employment rather than the adoption of innovative ways to increase output. Of course, given the lack of aggregate demand in the economy, the incentive for innovation would appear to be very low.

We are 100 percent in agreement with those who view productivity as the key driver of economic success and growth. Many of the prescriptions that we will offer later in this book will be aimed at boosting US productivity. We are just less sanguine than some on the United States' current potential for productivity growth. Without some changes, we cannot expect another productivity surge to come to the rescue.

SEEK SALVATION IN SERVICES

One theory of economic development, advanced by sociologist Daniel Bell in 1973, argues that economies go through natural progressions of development from agriculture to manufacturing to services.[25] From this perspective, the decline in manufacturing in the United States is a natural and healthy transition to a "post-industrial" society dominated by "knowledge work." It is a perspective that first gained popularity in the 1980s during the first wave of competitiveness debates. (In 1983, *Forbes* magazine advocated that "instead of following the Pied Piper of 'reindustrialization,' the US should be concentrating its efforts on strengthening its services."[26]) More recent proponents of this view include Michael Porter, our Harvard colleague and one of the most respected authorities on competitiveness.[27] He has argued:

Services are where the high value is today, not in manufacturing.
Manufacturing stuff per se is relatively low value. That is why it is
being done in China or Thailand. It's the service functions of
manufacturing that are where the high value is today, and that is what
America can excel in if we have the right kind of workforce and we
have the right kind of environment. We have to stop this notion [of
believing] that manufacturing is [essential]. It's a real problem because
it distorts our thinking.[28]

Proponents of such post-industrial views take comfort in the fact that services as a percentage of total economic activity (GDP) tend to increase as economies mature and develop. There is a relatively strong correlation at the country level between GDP per capita and percentage of GDP accounted for by services. And as we see in the United States, almost all net employment growth over the past decade has been in services, not manufacturing.

Because we will be devoting a significant part of later chapters to debunking this "forget manufacturing" argument, we only summarize our critique here. First, it is a huge leap of faith to interpret the correlation between the service intensity of an economy and growth in GDP per capita as causal. Indeed, it is very likely that the causality runs the opposite way: greater wealth and development tend to lead to great *consumption* of services. Retail, wholesale, transportation, entertainment, and personal services (e.g., legal, accounting, real estate brokerage, health care, personal care) all tend to grow as income levels rise. (Consider that there is not much retail shopping in very undeveloped economies.) And because many services have to be consumed locally, local consumption of services leads to increased local production of services. Consistent with this logic, the data analysis of Spence and Hlatshwayo shows that most growth in US employment in the past decades has occurred in nontradable service sectors. In addition, there are plenty of examples of countries with high GDP per capita and strong manufacturing sectors (Germany and Switzerland, to name two) to make us leery of any simple argument about the primacy of services over manufacturing.

Finally, we believe this perspective is blinded by some distorted views on the realities of manufacturing, its place in a "knowledge economy," and its contribution to innovation. Too often, services are equated with "knowledge work" and manufacturing is stereotyped as low-value-added "grunge" work. Generalizations in either direction are dangerous. Not all services are "burger-flipping"; there are plenty of high-value-added, high-skilled service jobs to be had. But the same is true of manufacturing. There are many high-value-added types of manufacturing that are just as much part of the knowledge economy as high-end services. In fact, in many contexts the real distinction between service and manufacturing is blurry. As we argue later, if the United States is serious about building its future economic growth around knowledge work and innovation, manufacturing has as important a role to play as services.

The focus of this chapter has been on how national competitiveness is really about the ability of people and organizations located in a geographic region to outperform the people and organizations in other regions both within the same country and in other parts of the world. To a significant degree, the economic prosperity of a country and its people depends on the competitiveness of these local industrial commons. We believe that the federal, state, and local governments in the United States and companies operating in the United States have not fully appreciated the importance of these local commons and have allowed many of them to decline even as governments and companies in other parts of the world have been building the capabilities of their local commons. In the next chapter we will explore the dynamics that lead to the establishment and growth of an industrial commons, and, conversely, can result in its decline.

CHAPTER 3

The Industrial Commons

What It Is and Why It Matters

Centuries ago a *commons* referred to the land where animals belonging to people in the community could graze. The commons did not belong to any one farmer; it was shared or collectively owned. All were better off for having access to it. Accordingly, everyone benefited when it was healthy, and everyone was hurt when it declined. Today, the term *commons* can be used to describe many public spaces, ranging from fishing grounds to public goods such as the education system and the transportation infrastructure.[1]

An analogous concept exists for industries. For any given industry—say, automobiles—companies in any given region usually draw from a common set of suppliers and human resources. While accessing these industrial resources is not free (as was true for grazing commons), they provide a shared benefit to multiple companies. If, for example, suppliers of precision machined parts become weaker technically or there are fewer first-rate mechanical engineers in the labor pool, all companies needing these capabilities suffer.

The existence or absence of a commons in a particular geography helps explain why some new industries take root in a particular area, whereas others have difficulty getting started. The development of early mass-production technologies in America in the 1800s is illustrative. During the American Revolution, small weapons such as muskets, rifles, and pistols were produced using the traditional approach: highly skilled craftsmen made them, which meant that no two weapons were exactly alike and parts were not interchangeable. This made it difficult to repair weapons in the field, which was a major problem for the resource-starved Continental Army.

That experience triggered the US government's fifty-year drive to push the federal armories at Springfield, Massachusetts, and Harpers Ferry, Virginia, to invest heavily in developing a new approach to manufacture weapons with interchangeable parts. It employed gauges, fixtures, inspection devices, and special-purpose machines for cutting and shaping wood and metal that were arranged in a sequence. This approach, which became known as the "American system of manufactures," also made possible huge increases in productivity.[2]

The federal armories and the privately owned Colt armory established in Hartford, Connecticut, in 1855 resulted in a commons that fed numerous other early manufacturing industries. For example, the network of toolmakers developed precision metalworking tools that were critical to the creation of sophisticated textile machinery.[3] Furthermore, the engineers and managers who grew up in the armories and sewing machine factories moved on to the furniture, lock, clock, bicycle, locomotive, and eventually automobile industries. Two of the largest locomotive makers of 1838, Lowell and Baldwin, were also textile-machine shops.[4] The Pratt & Whitney Company started out making tools for companies that manufactured gun-making machines and sewing machines and eventually moved into the manufacture of aircraft engines.[5]

Understanding Industry Linkages

Even as the rise of a commons can support the creation and growth of numerous industries, the decline of a sector of the commons can set off a negative chain reaction throughout a multitude of industries. To understand why, we need to understand the linkages between industries.

In the 1950s, Wassily Leontief developed the first method for creating input–output tables to track the flows of goods and services throughout an entire economy, a feat that earned him the Nobel Prize in economic science. These tables clearly show that some sectors have stronger supply–demand linkages than others. For instance, an increase in demand for computers will tend to spur semiconductor output more than, say, wheat output. The lesson of input–output analysis is that you can't judge the overall economic impact of a given sector just by looking at that sector. Some sectors have greater leverage through their input–output connections than others.

However, these tables do not take into account the fact that knowledge, intellectual property, and information can also flow across sectors. Such flows are particularly important when it comes to spurring innovation across sectors. For instance, an analysis of the automobile industry's key physical inputs in the 1980s would have shown very strong linkages with the steel, precision machined parts, and plastics industries, but it would have completely missed the fact that advances in semiconductors, software, and computers would revolutionize both the design process and the content of automobiles. Today, electronics account for about one-third of the cost of materials and labor in producing an automobile.[6]

Beneath the surface of *every* product is not just a set of physical components but also an even deeper set of hidden technical and organizational capabilities that enabled the creation, production, and delivery of that product. This chapter was typed on a MacBook

Pro notebook computer that is an embodiment of a whole constellation of capabilities: industrial design and software engineering; the engineering and manufacturing capabilities to produce the display; the lithography, etching, and related processing capabilities that produced the semiconductors; the high-precision molding capabilities that shaped the keys; the aluminum forming and polishing capabilities that formed the case; and so on.

What makes things interesting is that these underlying capabilities are not static. They evolve, and new ones emerge to change the possibilities of what a product can do (again, consider the impact of software on automobiles). Once we begin to consider these underlying networks of capabilities, we realize the somewhat obvious fact that innovation in any one industry can never really be viewed as isolated from what happens in other sectors. In fact, it is hard to think of any important innovation in history that occurred in a vacuum.

Innovation in steam locomotives required both scientific insights from the field of thermodynamics and advances in precision machine tools that came from the textile machinery industry. Advances in machine tools required dramatic improvements in the production of high-strength steel (to produce cutting tools that would not dull quickly). But as these became available, machine-tool manufacturers encountered another bottleneck: the existing motors were not powerful enough to fully exploit the greater cutting potential of high-strength steel.[7] The personal computer is the result of technical advances in several areas, including digital logic (microprocessors), semiconductor memories, software, high-precision manufacturing (for disk drives), and displays. Innovation in the drug industry requires advances in genetic profiling, clinical sciences, diagnostics, and so on. Today, the ability of electric vehicles to replace vehicles with gasoline-fueled combustion engines hinges on whether we can solve a host of complementary problems involving batteries (power/weight ratio, capacity, recharge time, packaging, safety, and cost) and can create an efficient infrastructure for recharging.

Industries, then, are not discrete economic units (although governments continue to measure them that way); rather, they are more akin to threads woven together into complex webs. As anyone who has ever pulled a loose thread on a sweater can tell you, the connections can lead to unpredictable results. Some connections between seemingly distant industries are actually quite close once we consider the underlying common capabilities.

For example, look at figure 3-1, a diagram of the capabilities underlying a diverse array of electronic products, from notebook computers and mobile phones to flat-screen TVs, solar panels, and lighting. As the diagram makes clear, there are interdependencies in the capabilities both produced and used across sectors. These interdependencies mean that the health of a given sector (in terms of its ability to innovate and grow) may be strongly shaped by its access to and connection with other sectors.

For example, chemical vapor deposition (CVD) is a way to produce thin films of high-purity materials, and it is a key process in the formation of transistors on the semiconductor microchips that are used in a host of electronic products. Knowledge of how to do this was vital to being able to form devices on glass for making flat-panel displays as well as depositing the layers of materials on thin-film solar panels. As semiconductor manufacturers needed to deposit more exotic materials, they came up with a variation known as metal-organic chemical vapor deposition (MOCVD)—basically CVD for metal-organic materials. This turned out to be the key process for making high-brightness LEDs, the technology that is revolutionizing energy-efficient lighting.

Innovation linkages can either be "supply push," "demand pull," or some combination. For instance, advances in computer-based engineering analysis and design tools and growth in computational power created opportunities for innovation in the design process of many industries, such as automobiles, aircraft, and electronic systems. Improvements in simulation capability *pushed* innovation in other

FIGURE 3-1

Interdependencies among electronic products

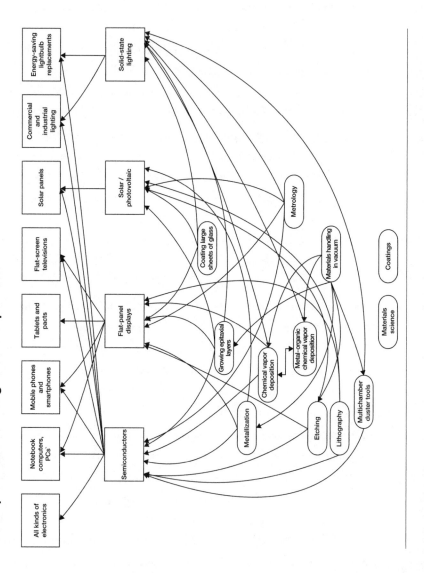

sectors. Advanced software design and analysis tools are at the forefront of improving the design and efficiency of wind turbines. In contrast, the consumer electronics industry's challenges of storing ever more power in smaller products *pulled* innovation in battery technology. Battery technology was (and still is) a bottleneck that needs to be overcome to improve product functionality. Clearly, the flows can go both ways. The aerospace industry is both a puller and pusher of innovation in high-temperature alloys and composites.

The notion that capabilities spill over sectors and that innovation capacity can be linked suggests that some capabilities play a more pivotal role in economic development than others. Broadly speaking, some sectors (because of the capabilities they either demand or create) have a greater potential to drive innovation in other sectors. Economists and economic historians use the term *general-purpose technologies* to describe capabilities that have the most pervasive impacts on economic activity.[8] Historically noteworthy examples of powerful general-purpose technologies include steam power (1700s), electrification (1800s), mechanization (mid- to late 1800s), chemical processing (late 1800s and early 1900s), digitization (mid- to late 1900s), and information technology and the Internet (late 1900s).

The economic development of individual countries has been strongly influenced by their participation in these technologies. The economic rise of England was strongly tied to it being the originator of the first industrial revolution (with steam power at its center). Germany's rise to economic prominence was tightly tied to its central role in the synthesis of organic chemicals and the development of corresponding manufacturing processes. Digitization, information technology, and the Internet figured prominently in the economic prowess of the United States in the post–World War II period.[9]

Although not as sweeping or apparent as the Internet or the steam engine, many other technologies affect innovation across sectors.

Consider semiconductor processing. Manufacturing a modern semi-conductor chip requires a set of processing capabilities in materials, patterning, deposition and removal processes, the modification of electrical properties, and the testing and packaging of finished chips. However, photovoltaic solar cells, flat-screen high-definition displays, and LED lighting use variations of the same core processing capabilities. Other examples of technologies or capabilities that have seeped into a broad range of sectors include precision machining, advanced composite materials, and engineering analysis software and simulation tools.

When Is Geographic Proximity Valuable?

The more important issue for forming government policies and companies' strategies is whether this seepage of know-how and capabilities is geographically bounded.

Let's take a concrete example from figure 3-1. Both semiconductors and displays draw from common capabilities in lithography. But for a semiconductor manufacturer to benefit from advances in lithography technology, does it need to be geographically close to where that capability is created? Or take the R&D and manufacturing example. Although it is true that R&D in biotech and manufacturing are tightly linked, does the geographic distance between R&D and manufacturing have an impact? Could a country specialize in biotech R&D and let other countries do the manufacturing (and vice versa)? The answers to these types of questions are critical to understanding both the strategy and the policy issues around the fortunes of specific sectors. If geographic boundaries are irrelevant—that is, all know-how travels very rapidly around the world—then just because sector A declines in a country does not mean that closely linked sector B in that country is in any danger of decline. But if distance does matter, then the health of sector A could have a big impact on the health of sector B. Thus, for purposes of both public policy and business strategy, it is important to understand precisely *when* distance matters.

The topic of geography and location in economics has a venerable history, dating back to one of the foundational figures in modern economics, Alfred Marshall, author of the 1890 work *Principles of Economics*.[10] One of Marshall's interests was in explaining what he called "the industrial district," or the geographic clustering of firms in the same industry. Marshall theorized three reasons why clustering occurs:

- *Labor market pooling:* Firms tend to locate where they can find the specialized talent they need, and people with specialized talents go where they can find the most employers requiring their skills.

- *Common infrastructure:* To run a business, you need access to other specialized complementary inputs such as supplies, equipment, and various services. Similar to the labor story, supply begets demand and demand begets further supply. You are not going to set up a shop to maintain semiconductor equipment in a locale with no semiconductor factories. And if you are thinking of building a semiconductor factory, you really do want to choose a place with ample choices of complementary service and equipment providers.

- *Spillovers:* Firms in the same industry generate know-how that they can't completely keep private. Some of their know-how becomes available to nearby firms through things such as the movement of workers. The potential for spillovers creates an incentive for other firms to locate nearby.

Nobel laureate Paul Krugman also has written about the importance of understanding "economic geography."[11] He argues that once manufacturers cluster in a manufacturing belt, it is not in anybody's interest to move out. The interactions of increasing returns from being in the cluster, more favorable transportation costs, and demand drive the growth and vitality of the region.

Do these geographic "agglomerating forces" still hold in today's world of open trade, lightning-fast communication networks, and rapid diffusion of know-how? Some argue no. Perhaps the most articulate proponent of this view is the journalist Thomas Friedman. In his book *The World Is Flat*, Friedman argues that a combination of institutional forces (the liberalization of economic systems and the vast reduction in trade barriers), technological changes (high-speed Internet and communication networks, software enabling collaboration), and economic forces (the emergence of major new markets in places such as China, India, and Brazil) are "flattening" the world, or essentially reducing the significance of distance.[12] It is certainly hard to argue that these kinds of changes have not shrunk the world and made distances less of a barrier. Today, an engineer using a relatively simple computer-aided design (CAD) system can design a product in India and then transmit that design to a manufacturing plant in China literally with the click of a mouse. Distance is no longer a great barrier to competition. This applies to companies and to people. As pointed out in chapter 2, if you are a software engineer living in Silicon Valley, make no mistake about it, you *are* competing with software engineers in India and Finland.

Friedman's argument is provocative and certainly has some merit. Let's compare the situation of an entrepreneur in eighteenth-century England with his counterpart in Silicon Valley today. During the eighteenth century, English entrepreneurs—such as Richard Arkwright, inventor of the spinning frame for spinning cotton into yarn—were coming up with all sorts of novel ideas for how machines could produce things faster, more efficiently, and more uniformly. These inventors really had no choice but to build their inventions locally. Fortunately, eighteenth-century England was chock-full of highly skilled craftsmen and machine builders, a legacy of the country's experience in clock making and shipbuilding.

Today, someone with a bright idea in Silicon Valley is not constrained by the available skills sets or complementary capabilities in Northern California; he or she can scour the globe for other pieces of the puzzle. Need some software engineered? Go to India. Need some low-cost manufacturing? Head to the Far East. You name it, you can find it somewhere, and you probably can do all this, globalists would have you believe, without leaving your room. Just surf the Web. This view of the world implies that if you live in the United States (or elsewhere) and are pretty creative, you do not need to worry about domestic manufacturing (or anything else for that matter).

Such a view is often used to justify, or at least make more palatable, the decline in manufacturing sectors in countries such as the United States. Although we certainly agree broadly that the world has become smaller and flatter in many respects, we think it is a dangerously gross oversimplification of the impact of distance and geography on innovation. Pankaj Ghemawat, in his book *World 3.0*, provides rigorous and clear data that in terms of trade, the world is far less flat than Friedman and other globalists claim.[13] For instance, Ghemawat points out that most trade is regional and that labor mobility across countries has actually declined over time, not increased. There are still plenty of visible and invisible barriers to trade.

Moreover, if we look around the world today, we actually see a picture that is eerily reminiscent of the world Marshall observed more than one hundred years ago: there is still a lot of "clustering," as Michael Porter calls these regional agglomerations of related industries.[14] Biotechnology and life sciences are heavily clustered in the greater Boston area, the San Francisco Bay Area, and San Diego. Semiconductor manufacturing is amassed in Taiwan, South Korea, Singapore, and Shanghai and Beijing, China. Financial services are concentrated in New York, London, Zurich, Tokyo, and, increasingly, Hong Kong. If we zoom in closer, we can also find clustering within countries and sectors at a more refined level. Italy is known for its high fashion shoes, but high-end shoe production is not evenly spread throughout Italy. It is concentrated in the Brenta Riviera (just south of Venice), Florence, Bologna, and Naples. Most of the world's low-end and midmarket shoes are produced in the Pearl River Delta of Guangdong province, China.

Clustering does not mean that firms in these sectors are not located in other parts of the world. It just captures the tendency. So, if you were to place a brightly colored dot on a map everywhere you found a firm associated with a certain industry, you would wind up with a map that looked very bright in some places, had some scattered dots in others, and was completely white in still others.

When it comes to exploiting knowledge and capability linkages across sectors, distance matters because not all knowledge and capability is easy, fast, or cheap to transmit rapidly. The Internet is a wonderful thing for information that can be codified into a digital format. One can send blueprints anywhere in the world at the click of a mouse.

However, blueprints and codified knowledge represent only a fraction of the total knowledge used and produced by organizations. Michael Polanyi, the twentieth-century philosopher of science and author of *Personal Knowledge*, argued that humans know a lot more than they can articulate, which he dubbed "tacit knowledge."[15] Take riding a bicycle. It is a skill we develop by practice; at some point, it becomes automatic. But as parents who have tried to teach their five-year-olds how to ride without training wheels can attest, communicating this knowledge of how to ride is devilishly difficult, if not impossible.

The same is true of organizations. Important knowledge is still carried around in the heads of people and in informal (almost invisible) routines used by organizations.[16] Consider the vaunted Toyota production system. For several decades, the Toyota production system was intensely studied by consultants and academics, and just about every major automobile company tried to copy it. (Toyota was happy to allow competitors to tour its factories.) Yet, persistent and large differences exist in the productivity and quality performance of automobile manufacturers.[17] It seems that there was important knowledge about the Toyota production system locked inside the heads of its employees that others couldn't access.

The Toyota example is an illustration of how tacitness constrains the diffusion of know-how across organizations. Tacitness also plays a role in constraining the diffusion of know-how across different geographies.[18] Because the transfer of tacit know-how requires face-to-face communication, its diffusion tends to be geographically bounded. The social networks through which know-how diffuses from scientist to scientist tend to be localized. Moreover, recent evidence suggests that the diffusion of tacit know-how is further constrained by the localized nature of many markets for talent. In a study of over sixty thousand US inventors, Stefano Breschi and Francesco Lissoni of Bocconi University found that only a small minority (less than 10 percent) ever relocate from one metropolitan area to another.[19]

Combining the notion of complements and geographic proximity suggests that opportunities for innovation for a company (or country) hinge partly on the availability of *local* complements. Some things you can buy from a distance; some things you can't. Strong complementarities in capabilities when combined with localized knowledge can give a region a powerful advantage in a next-generation industry and can block others from getting into the game. When these two conditions of strong complementarity and strong economies of geographic co-location are present, the resulting set of sectors forms what we call an *industrial commons.*

The Delicate Equilibrium of the Industrial Commons

As in an ecosystem found in nature, each "species" in an industrial commons (rivals, suppliers, customers, workers, and institutions such as universities) must find it advantageous to remain part of the community.[20] In economic terms, they must capture *private returns:* the benefits that accrue to an individual or to a firm from its own actions or investments. So, for instance, if General Motors (GM) invests in R&D to create a new fuel-efficient vehicle, and that vehicle does well in the marketplace, the profits flowing to GM are its private returns. The opportunity for private returns in excess of the cost of capital is the primary driver of investment decisions in market economies.

An ecosystem functions because each species contributes resources that provide benefits to others. In economic terms, these are called *social returns.* Ecosystems (in nature and economies) reach equilibrium when each species is contributing enough resources to sustain the population of the rest of the ecosystem.

As has been long known in economics, however, investments often generate returns that are not fully appropriable by the investing firm. Some economic benefits spill over to others. These are the social returns. Employee movement from firm to firm is a key channel of social returns. When a GM employee—who gained his skills thanks to investments by GM in, say, training or R&D projects—leaves GM to go to Ford, know-how flows from GM to Ford. Suppliers are another conduit. Suppliers that gain production experience supplying something to one company can utilize that experience to supply other companies. In many industries, such as flat-panel displays and semiconductors, tool suppliers (and tools that embody know-how) are principal conduits for disseminating process know-how among firms.

Another mechanism for social returns is *shared complementary assets.* A shared complementary asset is a resource (e.g., a supplier) or pool of resources (e.g., a supply of skilled labor) whose value increases with the number of users. There are many examples in which the presence of a critical mass of local buyers of a product or service is needed to induce supply. For instance, in contexts in which suppliers face high fixed costs, operate processes with high minimum efficient scale, and sell products or services that are not easily transported far away, these suppliers can only afford to stay in business if some threshold number of local customers buy from them. No one company has an incentive to buy more than it thinks it needs, but as a group, they need to provide enough demand to keep the supplier in business. In essence, each customer is paying for part of the fixed-cost base that benefits its rivals as well. Had GM been allowed to collapse in 2008, the collateral damage to its supply chain could have also been felt by Ford (which shared many of the same suppliers). The supply chain was a shared complementary asset that needed demand from both Ford and GM to survive.

Note that companies that operate in a commons realize that they are providing benefits to others. They recognize that the know-how, skills, and capabilities they create are absorbed by others, including competitors. They recognize that by providing demand for suppliers, they help suppliers reduce costs, which also benefits their rivals. But they also recognize that these benefits run both ways and they get to free-ride on the efforts of others. The CEO of one Boston-area biotech firm mentioned to us that he was thrilled when a major pharmaceutical company decided to make a multibillion-dollar investment in new laboratories in Cambridge. Whereas some of his counterparts at other companies worried that this new behemoth would make an already tight market for scientists even tighter and they could lose key talent, this CEO was delighted because it meant there was going to be a vast new pool of scientists coming to the area, providing his firm with another place from which to recruit talent.

Although companies are aware that they create social returns for others in the commons, these generally do not figure into the calculus of their decisions. Firms only really care about the private returns, and thus as long as private returns exceed their cost of capital, they will continue to make these investments even if they also happen to generate large spillover benefits to others. What determines whether a commons stays together is the private returns garnered by its members, not the social returns.

An industrial commons represents a delicate ecosystem. If one type of member (e.g., an important set of suppliers) begins to decline in number, the withdrawal of those resources from the system can lead to a decline in the viability of other members. This happens in nature. For instance, if the bee population declines, the flower population is affected. This may lead to less fruit production, which will then negatively affect species that rely on the fruit for food. A similar dynamic can grip industrial commons. In nature, the decline of an ecosystem is often triggered by an exogenous event (e.g., a random drop in temperature that, say, reduces the bee population). In the case of an industrial commons, if private returns from belonging to the commons drop below some threshold (usually the long-term cost of capital of some group of firms), those members may leave the commons. If their exodus reduces the benefits of staying in the commons for other firms, then a negative dynamic can set in, and the commons begins to erode. We will explore this issue in great detail in chapter 5.

This chapter has highlighted the interconnectedness and the broad reach of an industrial commons. We intentionally focused many of our examples on manufacturing. In some of the examples (e.g., the important role that the commons for the production of small weapons played in the rise of a number of other major industries in the United States), it was clearly important for R&D and manufacturing to be geographically close to each other. In other industries (e.g., semiconductors), however, such proximity seemed unnecessary. This raises a central question: when do R&D and manufacturing have to be near each other in order to innovate and when do they not? That is the topic of the next chapter.

CHAPTER 4

When Is Manufacturing
Critical to Innovation?

The role that manufacturing plays in the economic well-being of a country has been the subject of a long-running debate among policy makers, scholars, and business executives. As we pointed out earlier, there is a large camp that contends that as long as Americans are doing the design and R&D (the high-value-added stuff), manufacturing is irrelevant. According to this line of thinking, the United States has a comparative advantage in innovation, and therefore it makes perfect economic sense to let other countries (or, to be more precise, workers in other countries) do the manufacturing. They argue that Americans are the entrepreneurs and the innovators; that's their comparative advantage, and therefore business and government leaders should not worry if manufacturing (even if highly complex) goes overseas. Indeed, many start-up American companies today have no trouble raising capital to perform R&D or engineering in the United States, but hit a roadblock if they want capital to build a factory in the United States. "No way," the venture capitalists say. "That should be outsourced to China, Mexico, India, or some other low-cost place."

This line of thinking is based on false premises about the divisibility of R&D and manufacturing in the innovation process. Just as manufacturing is too often inaccurately cast as low-skill, low-wage grunge work, it is similarly viewed as outside the innovation process. Say the word *innovation* and the following images pop up: brightly lit, airy studios (with the obligatory foosball table tucked in the corner); designers clad in T-shirts and guzzling Starbucks coffee; geeky engineers whose eyes are fixed on the screens of their high-powered CAD workstations; entrepreneurs in their twenties or thirties scribbling their concepts on napkins over lunch; and so on.

These activities are *not* innovation. Innovation is not a laboratory discovery, a concept, or a prototype. Innovation is the process of taking a new idea or concept to the market. The hot new product—the iPad, the Kindle, the breakthrough cancer drug, the new electric vehicle—gets the headlines. But often, not far beneath the surface lies the development of complex, precision manufacturing processes that must be capable of producing millions of units at economically feasible costs with extraordinarily high quality. If this part of the innovation process fails, you don't have an innovation; you had a promise.

We do not argue that manufacturing is always deeply intertwined with the innovation process. Sometimes it is; sometimes it is not. The degree of interdependence between R&D and manufacturing is the critical contingency we must assess in answering the question, When is manufacturing important to a nation's innovative capacity? *Under specific circumstances*, the design of products is so tightly intertwined with the design and operation of their corresponding manufacturing processes that it makes little, if any, sense to talk about them separately. The capacity to solve production problems is as important to the value of the innovation as is the ability to select the right product characteristics or design features. Under these circumstances, weakness in manufacturing will ultimately erode capabilities for innovation. In contrast, where product

R&D is fully separable from process innovation and manufacturing, then the case for domestic manufacturing (in terms of maintaining the health of a country's innovative capacity) is much weaker.

Determining R&D and Manufacturing Interdependence

How can you know whether a given product has a high or low degree of R&D–manufacturing interdependence and whether moving production halfway around the world, far from R&D operations, will hurt a company's (and country's) ability to innovate over the long term? You need to look at two things: the ability of R&D and manufacturing to operate independently of each other (the degree of modularity[1]) and the maturity of the manufacturing-process technology.[2]

Modularity

When R&D and manufacturing are highly modular, variability in the major characteristics of the product (features, functionality, aesthetics, and so on) aren't determined by the production processes, and the two activities can be located far apart without any consequences. When modularity is low, the product design can't be fully codified in written specifications, and design choices influence manufacturing choices (and vice versa) in subtle and difficult-to-predict ways. In these cases keeping manufacturing near R&D is valuable.

A simple example of high modularity is the creation and production of this book. In writing it, we engaged in a "design" process. But this process is utterly independent of the process by which the physical or digital page you may be reading was produced. As authors, we did not have to care about the production process that was going to be used to produce these pages. Similarly, the people responsible for producing these pages did not need to worry about our content.

At the other end of the modularity spectrum are the processes for producing recombinant DNA protein drugs. There, product development and manufacturing are closely intertwined. In biotech drugs, R&D involves both identifying products (protein structures) that have desirable therapeutic properties (reducing inflammation, for example) and designing a process capable of making that specific protein. A subtle change in the process (for instance, a slight change in the composition of the production media) can cause the production of a different protein. Moreover, not all the critical process variables that influence the product are precisely understood. Thus there is a lot of iteration (trial and error) between R&D and manufacturing in the development process. If you just throw the product over the wall to manufacturing, there is a good chance you won't be able to scale up production.

Two basic questions will help you determine the degree of modularity. The first is, how much must product designers know about the production process to carry out their task? In some contexts, such as biologics and advanced materials, every conceivable product design requires a unique manufacturing process. Therefore designers cannot do their jobs without deeply understanding the process choices. In these contexts, product innovation often involves process innovation.

At the other extreme are contexts in which it's technically and economically feasible to use the same process technology to manufacture just about any product design. That means designers can blissfully create without thinking about—or even understanding—the process. Writers of text, software, and music operate with this freedom.

Some industries lie in between; they have developed formal approaches for incorporating process considerations into product development. They establish "design rules"—a set of specifications that will work with a particular process. As long as designers stay within those boundaries, they can be pretty confident that the given manufacturing process will work. In general, process constraints intensify as product designs move closer to or try to go beyond those boundaries.

The second question is, How difficult is it for a product designer to get relevant information about the production process? Process technologies run along a spectrum from pure art to pure science. Processes at the pure-art end have unclear and difficult-to-describe parameters. To understand them, you need to see them—and even then, they may be hard to replicate. In these contexts, product innovation typically requires intense iteration between product and process development and feedback during actual production.

Maturity

By maturity we mean how much a process has evolved rather than the age of a technology, although obviously the two tend to be correlated. Immature processes offer the greatest opportunities for improvement. In the 1960s, after scientists at DuPont first discovered Kevlar, the polyaramid fiber used in body armor and other high-strength applications, the company spent fifteen years and $500 million commercializing the manufacturing process and learning how to weave the material. As processes mature, the opportunities for improvement usually become more incremental.

When manufacturing technologies are immature, companies can thrive by focusing on process innovation. In the early 1980s, Japanese semiconductor companies exploited many opportunities for improving manufacturing techniques that their US competitors had missed and took a commanding position in memory chips. Today, in sectors such as advanced flat-panel displays, biologics, and advanced materials, the process-technology frontiers are moving so quickly that world-class innovation is a must to stay in the game.

Viewed through the modularity–process maturity lens, relationships between manufacturing and innovation fall into four quadrants (figure 4-1), each of which is discussed below.

PURE PRODUCT INNOVATION

Here, the value of tightly integrating product innovation with manufacturing is low, and the opportunities for improving processes are few. Outsourcing manufacturing makes a lot of sense.

Many segments of the semiconductor industry fit into this quadrant. This explains why there is a thriving sector of "fabless"

FIGURE 4-1

The modularity–maturity matrix

	High	
Process maturity: the degree to which the process has evolved	**Process-embedded innovation** Process technologies, though mature, are still highly integral to product innovation. Subtle changes in process can alter the product's characteristics in unpredictable ways. *Design cannot be separated from manufacturing.* EXAMPLES Craft products, high-end wine, high-end apparel, heat-treated metal fabrication, advanced materials fabrication, specialty chemicals	**Pure product innovation** The processes are mature, and the value of integrating product design with manufacturing is low. *Outsourcing manufacturing makes sense.* EXAMPLES Desktop computers, consumer electronics, active pharmaceutical ingredients, commodity semiconductors
	Process-driven innovation Major process innovations are evolving rapidly and can have a huge impact on the product. The value of integrating R&D and manufacturing is extremely high. *The risks of separating design and manufacturing are enormous.* EXAMPLES Biotech drugs, nanomaterials, OLED and electrophoretic displays, superminiaturized assembly	**Pure process innovation** Process technology is evolving rapidly but is not intimately connected to product innovation. *While locating product design near manufacturing is not critical, proximity between process R&D and manufacturing is.* EXAMPLES Advanced semiconductors, high-density flexible circuits
	Low	

Low ⟶ High

Modularity: the degree to which information about product design can be separated from the manufacturing process

semiconductor firms (such as Qualcomm) that specialize in design but own no fabrication (i.e., production) facilities, and a thriving sector of firms that just manufacture (such as Taiwan Semiconductor Manufacturing Company) but don't do design.

PURE PROCESS INNOVATION

Here, process technology is ripe for improvements and advancing rapidly but isn't intimately connected to product innovation. Neither vertical integration nor locating design near manufacturing is critical, and it makes sense for specialized contract manufacturers to provide custom production to firms that focus on design. However, before ceding manufacturing to others, companies should keep in mind that process innovation can be a significant source of value in these contexts.

Advanced semiconductors fit into this quadrant. Companies can design advanced chips without operating their own manufacturing plants because design rules have emerged in the industry. However, since advanced-chip production yields are relatively low, significant process innovations can still improve the business's economics. Most stand-alone mechanical components fall into this category as well. If you are making a high-density flexible circuit, there can be a great deal of process innovation in the manufacturing process. But design rules embodied in the engineering specification ensure independence of the design from manufacture.

PROCESS-EMBEDDED INNOVATION

In this quadrant process technologies, although mature, are highly integral to the product-innovation process. Small changes in the process can alter the characteristics and quality of the product in unpredictable ways. Product innovation is incremental and comes from tweaking the process. (Think: wine.) Therefore the value of keeping R&D and manufacturing organizationally integrated and geographically close is high.

Many traditional creative businesses—such as high-end fashion—fit into this quadrant. With luxury apparel, how a fabric is cut or how a seam is sewn can affect the way a garment drapes in subtle ways that matter. One European producer of luxury apparel that we studied has worked only with local fabric suppliers because the suppliers' manufacturing engineers and the company's product designers need to exchange information almost constantly.

PROCESS-DRIVEN INNOVATION

In sectors developing breakthrough products at the frontiers of science, the major process innovations are evolving rapidly. Because even minor changes in the process can have a huge impact on the product, the value of closely integrating R&D and manufacturing is extremely high, and the risks of separating them are enormous. Managers, investors, and analysts haven't always recognized this danger. Viewing manufacturing as a distraction and a drain on capital, they often push companies in this quadrant to outsource production or move it to lower-cost locations far away from R&D. The results can be disastrous because, to put it simply, when you lose your manufacturing competence, you lose the ability to create new commercially viable products.

Biotechnology offers a good example.[3] Drugs derived from genetic engineering techniques are large protein molecules that are too complex to be chemically synthesized—the approach used to make drugs for over a century. Without major advances in process technology (such as mammalian cell culture processes), blockbuster drugs such as Amgen's erythropoietin for treating anemia or Roche/Genentech's Herceptin, a therapy for breast cancer, would never have made it out of the laboratory. One of Genentech's first employees had a manufacturing background, and early on, the company closely integrated the work of its scientists with its manufacturing operations.[4] Amgen built one of the strongest process-science groups in the industry. The ability to scale these highly delicate processes can determine the difference between commercial success and failure.

Intel is another company that understands the links between process innovation and product innovation. Its process R&D and manufacturing capabilities have opened up new avenues for product innovation. We noted earlier that many semiconductor companies no longer manufacture their own chip designs. Relying on third-party contractors makes perfect sense if your design strategy is not to push the process envelope. But Intel's strategy is to push that envelope—to pack more performance onto ever-smaller, denser, and more-complex chips. A case in point is its most advanced microprocessors (codenamed "Ivy Bridge"), which Intel launched in the spring of 2012. They employ a new transistor technology known as "fin" field effect transistors (FinFETs), which relies on microscopic raised three-dimensional finlike structures made of silicon to enable the chips to operate at a faster speed than existing microprocessors but with the same or lower power consumption. Competitors are believed to be as many as four to five years behind Intel in being able to introduce similar chips.[5] Why? The manufacture of these chips requires a new twenty-two-nanometer process to make the chips. Because Intel controls its own manufacturing and developed a proprietary process to make the chips, its chip designers could better understand the opportunities and limitations of the new process technology than their counterparts at rival companies that had outsourced manufacturing.

So When Does Manufacturing Matter?

Our framework can help identify when America and companies operating in America should worry that a decline in US manufacturing will have negative consequences for the country's and companies' ability to innovate, and when they should not. If a product falls into either the upper-left quadrant (process-embedded innovation) or lower-left quadrant (process-driven innovation) of our matrix, then the argument that it is fine to focus on product R&D and let others do the manufacturing is wrong. In that kind of context, the movement of manufacturing away from the United States will eventually pull R&D with it.

Crucially, the answer may be different for a final product and its individual components. Take the Apple iPad. It falls into the pure-product-innovation quadrant, which explains why the highly successful product could be designed in California while many of its components are designed and produced in Asia, where final assembly also occurs. But a number of the iPad's components (e.g., lithium ion batteries and the touch screen) fall into different quadrants, where it's important for R&D and manufacturing to be located near each other. What is more, the location of those R&D and manufacturing capabilities in other countries means that the future products that need those capabilities will come from those countries, too.

This might sound very hypothetical, but it's not. We have seen this movie many times before. One case in point is the rise of digital photography. Contrary to lore, Kodak was not asleep at the birth of the digital revolution. Its people had long been working on digital technologies, and in 1994, it produced one of the first consumer digital cameras (for Apple). About thirty years prior, Kodak had stopped making anything but the simplest of film cameras. (This strategy was dictated by the seemingly impeccable logic that because film was very profitable and cameras were not, it made no financial sense to produce cameras.) The camera industry moved to Japan as companies such as Nikon, Canon, Olympus, Asahi Pentax, and Minolta took over the business.

Initially, Kodak planned to maintain R&D, design, final assembly, and testing in the United States and purchase components from Japanese suppliers. A visit to Japan by one of us (Willy), who was a senior Kodak executive at the time, quickly revealed the problem with this strategy. Digital cameras were pretty complex. They combined optical, mechanical, and electronic engineering skills, and many of the manufacturing processes were evolving rapidly. This meant that the designs of the product and processes were not modular; the product fell into the process-embedded-innovation quadrant. Small changes made to the design could dramatically alter the ease of assembly or the quality of the image produced. This integrality of product R&D with process R&D and manufacturing made it crucial to have all the functions geographically close to one another so that engineers could go back and forth to the plant.

This is exactly what the city of Suwa in Japan's Nagano prefecture provided. It was a vibrant commons for cameras (especially compact models) and small, portable consumer electronics that boasted a strong local network of suppliers with deep technical expertise that had worked together in the past. In a business such as digital cameras, where product lives are short and time to market is critical, the ability of the members of the commons to collectively develop new products quickly was an enormous advantage. Members included Seiko Epson, which made watches, printers, and tiny electronic displays; Nittō Kōgaku, which produced zoom lenses and a variety of optical components; Sony and Matsushita, which made CCD sensors that digitally captured images; and other companies that made circuit boards, injection-molded plastics and the molds for making plastic parts, tiny machined parts, shutter buttons, camera electronic flash tubes, and rechargeable batteries. The region was also home to Chinon Industries, a manufacturer of cameras and lenses in which Kodak had purchased a stake.

A designer sitting in Rochester, New York, where there was no camera or consumer electronics industry, was at a serious disadvantage. With product cycles of less than one year, flying teams back and forth between Rochester and Suwa wasn't feasible: aside from being expensive, it consumed too much time. In 1998, Kodak had no choice but to shut down a highly automated assembly line for cameras that it had built in Rochester and, with the exception of some software operations, relocate its digital-camera-design activities to Japan.

This chapter should have convinced you that the decline of a country's commons is a serious problem for the innovative potential of a country. Now let's examine both the decisions and circumstances that gave rise to a unique and fertile commons in the United States and those that have eroded it in the last four decades.

CHAPTER 5

The Rise and Decline of the American Industrial Commons

Three forces play a role in the rise and decline of an industrial commons: government policies (e.g., funding for research), corporate strategies and management decisions (e.g., R&D investment, location decisions), and exogenous circumstances (e.g., wars, the size of the national market). This chapter examines how these forces have interacted to drive the rise of the American industrial commons and then contributed to its decline. Our goal is not to provide an encyclopedic history; rather, it is to provide a context for the prescriptions we offer in chapters 6 and 7.

The Rise

As noted in chapter 3, the first American industrial commons—that associated with mass production—had its roots in the decision of the US military to establish armories and have them produce weapons with interchangeable parts. This resulted in the development of the American system of manufactures: single-purpose specialized machines arranged in a sequential production system that yielded vast increases in productivity.[1] Together with the private Colt armory established in Hartford, Connecticut, in 1855, the armories established a commons that fed numerous other early manufacturing industries: sewing machines, textile machinery, furniture, locks, clocks, bicycles, locomotives, machine tools, and eventually automobiles.

A large national market also played a prominent role in building a commons for mass production. Part of that was due to circumstance—the tremendous growth in the size of the United States from its founding through the nineteenth century. But government policies were also responsible for the development of a bona fide national market. The creation of national transportation and communication systems is a case in point. In the 1860s, the Pacific Railroad Acts gave 103 million acres of public lands to companies for the development of a national railroad network.[2] The railroads, and later the telegraph networks that followed the tracks, became the arteries of a truly large domestic American market and drove a second industrial revolution in the United States.[3] (The funding of the national highway system, which began during the Eisenhower administration in the 1950s, is another example.) The rapidly growing national market enticed private companies to make large-scale investments in production and distribution (and later in R&D).[4] In contrast, the growth of the European market was impeded until deep into the twentieth century by its fragmented state—the result of cultural, language, and trade barriers between the nations of Europe; political and military conflicts; and the lack of a single currency.

The development of the US industrial commons also got a huge boost from an American organizational innovation: the formation of the modern, professionally managed corporation.[5] As business historian Alfred Chandler documented, it was the formation of the modern corporate structure—characterized by the separation of ownership from management, the creation of governance structures (such as boards of directors) and hierarchical management structures, and the rise of a professional managerial class—that made possible the investments in large-scale manufacturing technology and distribution capable of serving the huge American market.[6]

The rise of a commons based on mass production capabilities in the United States would be hard to imagine without one of the three key factors at work. Government initially planted the seeds through investments in armories. The circumstance of a large domestic market (unified by a growing network of railroads and telegraph communications) created opportunity to exploit economies of scale. But to reap these economies of scale, massive investment from private enterprises was necessary; it was the invention of a novel organizational form—the modern corporation—that enabled the required investments in technological and organizational capability.[7] These same conditions were not present in Europe. This interplay of private sector, government sector, and economic circumstance is a theme that repeats itself in the emergence of a technology-based commons in the years after World War II.

The Seeds of a Technology-Based Manufacturing Commons

The emphasis that Americans have placed on education, dating back to colonial times, also contributed to the rise of American dominance in technology industries. Universal elementary and secondary education spread throughout the United States in the nineteenth century. The Morrill Act of 1862 (also known as the Land Grant College Act) provided a major boost to higher scientific and technical education in America. It fostered the establishment of institutions in each state that would educate people in agriculture, home economics, the mechanical arts, and other "practical" professions. And in response to the growing needs of the railroad, telegraph, and other industries, schools such as the Massachusetts Institute of Technology (MIT) and the Stevens Institute of Technology were established and engineering curricula were added at elite institutions such as Yale and Columbia.[8] During the years prior to World War II, American universities also came into their own in several other fields of applied science, such as aeronautical engineering.

The creation of corporate research laboratories in the late nineteenth and early twentieth century by US companies such as DuPont, GE, AT&T, and Westinghouse was another important development in the evolution of the American industrial commons.[9] (These companies were following the lead of large German chemical and pharmaceutical companies.) Although there were many independent inventors and independent laboratories during this period (e.g., Edison's Menlo Park laboratory), companies began to create their own in order to achieve better integration between research and their commercial activities. They also began to see research as a possible defensive weapon against competition. AT&T, for instance, established its labs in response to the threat posed by radio to its telephone business. An increasing number of American corporations began to consider innovation to be an important element of corporate strategy, and at some companies (e.g., DuPont), scientific research capabilities became a core foundation of their businesses.[10]

Government policies—including antitrust and patent laws and the courts' enforcement of those laws—also encouraged the trend of relying on innovation and scientific research to compete.[11] A stringent interpretation of the Sherman Antitrust Act by the US courts in the late nineteenth century made competitors that had struck cooperative agreements to control prices or production the targets of civil prosecution. Court rulings in the late nineteenth and early twentieth centuries that strengthened the ability of companies to use patents to protect and license their discoveries also helped corporations view R&D as a potent competitive weapon.

Finally, companies began to realize that in order to make use of the growing body of external science related to their businesses, they needed internal capabilities in science and research.[12] That is, by establishing strong internal research capabilities, they were better able to absorb and exploit the know-how being created in the broader commons.

The unique global competitive position of American firms leading up to World War II arose from their ability to marry mass production and distribution methods to organized, science-based research.[13] This was a reflection of organizational and managerial capabilities as much as anything, and ability to exploit inventions and innovations on a large scale. This was especially the case in the chemical and electrical industries, as we have pointed out, as companies such as DuPont, GE, Westinghouse, and AT&T were able to generate a flow of new ideas out of their research labs and translate them into high-volume products that earned high returns that could be reinvested.

The Rise of the Post–World War II Technology-Based Industrial Commons

By sparking enormous public and private investments in America's production capacity and technological capabilities and devastating much of the industrial bases of Europe and Asia, World War II set the stage for a long period of US economic dominance. The war had a transformative effect on how science was viewed in the United States. Most of the country's scientific and technical resources were mobilized in support of the war effort, and academics worked side by side with scientists and engineers from industry. Their innovations included radar, the proximity fuse, antibiotics, the electronic computer, and the atomic bomb. The American public viewed scientists as heroes who played a critical role in winning the war.[14]

A year before the end of the war, President Franklin Delano Roosevelt asked Vannevar Bush, his wartime director of the Office of Scientific Research and Development, to look ahead to the role of science in peacetime.[15] In his report, which later became published as *Science: The Endless Frontier*, Bush argued that the R&D capability assembled during the war should not be allowed to atrophy, and that the federal government should take responsibility to support basic research. FDR died before the end of the war, but his successors and Congress heeded Bush's advice. In the decades following the war, there was a surge in federal funding for basic and applied scientific research—through both existing departments such as the Pentagon (which was engrossed in the arms race with the Soviet Union) and new agencies such as the National Science Foundation and the National Institutes of Health (figure 5-1).

FIGURE 5-1

US federal government spending on basic and applied research (in billions of constant 2000 dollars)

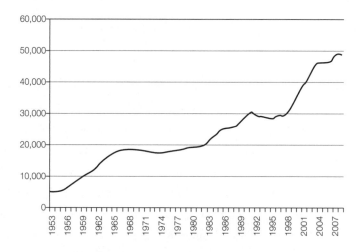

Source: Data from National Science Board, *Science and Engineering Indicators 2010* (Arlington, VA: National Science Foundation, 2010).

The postwar era also witnessed tremendous growth in the number of Americans with college degrees as a result of the GI Bill and the affluence spreading across the country. The nation's pool of scientists and engineers vastly increased, and they had little trouble finding jobs thanks to the expanding university research system, government-financed research, and, last but far from least, demand from companies that were establishing or enlarging their research programs (figure 5-2).[16]

The military's needs spawned whole new fields of technological capabilities. For instance, the need for reliable electronics in intercontinental ballistic missiles (ICBMs) was crucial to the development of integrated circuits by companies such as Texas Instruments. The need to supply electric power to satellites operating in space drove the early development of solar panels. And the F101 jet engine, designed for the B-1 bomber, was the source of the core "hot section" of the CFM56 family of commercial engines that today power Boeing 737s and Airbus A320s.

FIGURE 5-2

Total corporate spending on R&D (in billions of constant 2000 dollars)

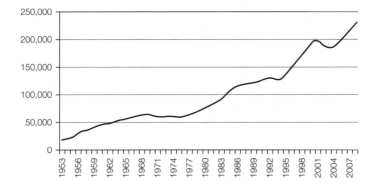

Source: Data from National Science Board, *Science and Engineering Indicators 2010* (Arlington, VA: National Science Foundation, 2010).

In the three decades after World War II, industrial research helped America to make products that could not be made anywhere else in the world. American firms were significantly ahead of their counterparts abroad in employing cutting-edge technologies that drew on new scientific frontiers, and their foreign subsidiaries often dominated their respective markets. It was an era of unquestioned American competitiveness.

The Tragedy of the Commons: Why America Is Losing Its Technology Leadership

We highlighted the decline of America's technological leadership and competitiveness in earlier chapters, using both aggregate statistics and specific cases studies. The case of semiconductors is illustrative of both the rise and the decline of a commons. Semiconductor-processing technology is a foundational capability that supports a broad range of sectors, including semiconductor chips, photovoltaic solar cells, LED lighting, and high-definition displays.

The semiconductor commons includes a broad array of people, firms, and capabilities. In addition to the people and firms engaged in the manufacture of chips, the members of the commons include the toolmakers; suppliers of materials such as pure silicon wafers, chemicals, and industrial gases; the people and firms who develop software for activities as varied as designing the chips, scheduling production, and testing the chips after they've been produced; and the researchers in materials science and device physics who do the foundational R&D, mostly at universities and leading-edge chip firms.

Thirty years ago America was the indisputable leader in semiconductor development and manufacturing.[17] The semiconductor commons was firmly rooted in the United States. The transistor, the integrated circuit, the dynamic random-access memory chip

(DRAM), and the microprocessor were all invented and first manufactured in the United States. All the key suppliers were in the
United States, because semiconductor pioneers such as IBM and
Texas Instruments made their own tools and pretty much did
everything.[18]

Slowly and inexorably, however, the US commons that supported
semiconductor manufacturing withered away. With the exception of
Intel, which flourished because of its powerful architectural franchise
in microprocessors, only the fabrication-less (fabless) design part of
the industry is still vibrant. Seventy percent of the current semiconductor foundry capacity in the world is in Taiwan, and almost all of
the rest is in Singapore, China, South Korea, and Japan. With the
exception of Micron Technology, nobody else builds DRAMs in the
United States; South Korea and Taiwan supply almost the entire
world market. There is no significant capacity in the United States
for the manufacture of flash memory.[19] Toolmakers such as Applied
Materials have been moving an increasingly larger proportion of their
tool assembly out of the United States. Some toolmakers (e.g.,
Kulicke & Soffa Industries) have even moved their headquarters from
America to Asia. Almost 100 percent of chip testing ("wafer prob-
ing") and packaging is performed outside the United States. There
are almost no domestic suppliers of chip-packaging materials.

The reason for this decline is a combination of aggressive foreign
competition and the failure of a number of parties to take responsibility for the long-term health of the commons. Federal and state
governments in the United States blithely ignored the fact that
lower taxes and more generous subsidies offered by other countries
made it hard for companies to justify building new multibillion-
dollar fabrication plants in the United States. American fabless
firms—those that design chips and outsource their production—did
not feel it was their responsibility to maintain a healthy foundry
sector in the United States and were happy to go to Asia for manufacturing. And finally, American chip manufacturers failed to keep

pace with the process capability, quality, cost, and flexibility of Japanese, Taiwanese, and South Korean firms.

The beginning of the decline can be traced to the 1970s, when Japan's Ministry of International Trade and Industry (MITI) launched a research initiative in the area of very large-scale integrated (VLSI) circuits. The principal goal of the VLSI project was to improve domestic capabilities for manufacturing semiconductors used in mainframe computers. Forty percent funded by the Japanese government, the program sought to strengthen the country's domestic industry through consolidation and restructuring, focusing on fine-line lithography, circuit design, wafer processing and testing, and computer-aided design. Five Japanese companies joined the project and were able to develop a set of capabilities.

Unlike in America, where demand for integrated circuits initially was driven by the military, demand in Japan was driven by the consumer electronics industry, which had already migrated to Japan, and by Nippon Telegraph and Telephone (NTT). Both had a huge need for DRAM chips. Therefore the Japanese focused on process-R&D-intensive products such as DRAMs and less-design-intensive products and emphasized superior manufacturing. In contrast, US companies didn't pay as much attention to manufacturing; consequently, their processes were not as good. Another big advantage for the Japanese industry was the presence of local suppliers of optical lithography tools, such as Canon and Nikon. The result of all the above: Japanese firms drove all American firms other than Texas Instruments, Micron, and IBM out of the DRAM segment, and the survival of American semiconductor toolmakers was very much in doubt.[20]

Salvation of a sort came in the form of a breakthrough that allowed the design of chips to be separated from the actual manufacturing. In the 1980s, researchers funded by the Defense Advanced Research Projects Agency (DARPA) came up with ways to establish design rules for semiconductor manufacturing so that chip designers could enter their designs into a computer, which would then spit out instructions that a factory could use to build the chips. Many US firms—including highly successful start-ups such as Qualcomm and NVIDIA—went fabless: they created chip designs and outsourced production to Asia, where governments, including Taiwan's and Singapore's, invested in R&D and offered incentives to encourage the establishment and growth of foundries that performed contract manufacturing. (Taiwan, whose contract semiconductor manufacturers include the Taiwan Semiconductor Manufacturing Company [TSMC] and the United Microelectronics Corporation [UMC], now accounts for about 70 percent of such capacity in the world; almost all of the rest is in Singapore, China, South Korea, and Japan.[21])

As the center of gravity of semiconductor manufacturing has moved east, so has the rest of the commons. Some US suppliers of semiconductor-production equipment, such as Applied Materials, KLA-Tencor, and Kulicke & Soffa, continue to be leaders in the industry. In order to be close to customers, however, Applied Materials increasingly assembles its tools and performs R&D in Asia, and Kulicke & Soffa moved its headquarters from Pennsylvania to Singapore. With the rise of China as a center for manufacturing electronics, even the fabless design firms have been shifting their resources to Asia in order to be closer to customers.

A handful of integrated design manufacturers (IDMs), such as Freescale Semiconductor and Texas Instruments, still do some manufacturing in the United States. However, the enormous costs of maintaining leading-edge semiconductor-manufacturing capabilities have caused almost all of these IDMs to choose a "fab-lite" strategy of continuing to run their older factories in America and outsource to Asian foundries their new, advanced processes.

Intel is the only large chip company that still does a large proportion of its manufacturing in the United States. Intel can continue to manufacture in America because it is a dominant player in the segment, the segment is highly profitable, and it must stay in the lead in process technology in order to maintain its competitive edge.

The decline of the semiconductor commons in the United States has been having a collateral impact on other industries as well. For example, the shift in production of semiconductor-manufacturing tools to Asia has dramatically reduced the need for precision machining in the San Francisco Bay area, causing a decline in the number of shops that do this kind of work. This decline has the potential to cause problems for other industries (e.g., aerospace, precision instruments) that depend on these suppliers.

The decline of the semiconductor commons resulted from the interplay of three forces: active government policies in regions such as Asia (and a lack of policies in the United States); changed circumstances (the shift in manufacturing assembly and supply chains to Asia, a change in technology that made it feasible to separate R&D and manufacturing); and private companies' strategies (decisions to go fabless and to source production from Asia). In the remainder of this chapter, we will focus on how these three forces have been reshaping the American industrial commons.

Changed Circumstances: A Highly Competitive World

Today's global economy is vastly different from the economic structure that prevailed during much of the post–World War II period (1945–1990). Prior to 1990, when US companies talked of "global competition," that meant incursions by Japanese or European companies into the United States, the core market for most American companies. Yes, American companies sold overseas, and multinationals had operated overseas for decades. But the focus for all but a few of the exceptionally global-minded companies was the US economy. Who could blame them? The United States was the world's largest market and the biggest source of growth and profits.

(Europe was fragmented and growing slowly, and Japan, with its import barriers, was impenetrable.) Markets outside Japan or Europe were generally categorized as "other" or "ROW" (rest of world). As for the competition, the Europeans generally excelled only at the higher end of markets (e.g., luxury autos such as BMW and Mercedes, or fashion). Only the Japanese were viewed as serious competitors in high technology and manufacturing.

That all started to change around 1990 with a structural shift: the entry of China, Russia and eastern Europe, Brazil, and India into the global picture. This had two effects. One was to dramatically expand the field of competition. No longer were American workers and American companies competing against traditional (and familiar) rivals from Japan and Europe. Hungry and aggressive competitors from unfamiliar places were kicking in the doors of the once-cosseted club of global "elites."

The vast supply of low-cost labor in these newcomer countries has been a powerful magnet that has been pulling US companies offshore. More important, as the skills of the workforces in those countries increase, and as those countries accumulate technological capabilities (which China is doing through large investments in R&D and technology transfer from Western companies), they will become more even more attractive locations. This is an important change because it means rethinking the assumption that these countries will be a competitive threat only to lower-value-added sectors (such as lower-skilled, labor-intensive manufacturing). It also means we can no longer assume that in contexts in which it is important to co-locate R&D and manufacturing, the balance will not tip in favor of putting *both* R&D and manufacturing offshore.

A second structural shift under way concerns the size of the market and opportunities for market growth. One of the great constants in the history of US economic development has been the potent advantage created by having a very large (and ultimately the largest) domestic market. As noted earlier, this provided both US and foreign companies with powerful incentives to build R&D, manufacturing, and distribution capabilities in the United States. America is still the world's single largest national economy (although the eurozone has approximately the same GDP), but it no longer is the fastest-growing market. That distinction goes to the so-called BRIC countries (Brazil, Russia, India, and China).

During the period from 2003 to 2008 (before the Great Recession struck the United States and Europe), China's economic growth averaged 10 percent per year, India's about 8 percent, and Russia's and Brazil's 6 percent and 4 percent, respectively.[22] In contrast, the US economy's average growth during the same period was 2.76 percent. Between 2000 and 2008, China alone contributed about 16 percent to global economic growth—more than any other single economy and more than all of the eurozone.[23] China is also fast becoming the largest market for automobiles, mobile phones, medical devices, factory equipment, and other products. This essentially means the United States has lost or is in the process of losing its "largest domestic market" advantage. Whereas once the size of the US market was a powerful magnet that attracted investment in its industrial commons, countries such as China, India, and Brazil now enjoy that advantage.

Another big change is that other nations have recognized the close ties between investments in R&D and education and economic and social benefits and have caught up with and, in many cases, surpassed the United States in the amounts they are plowing into these areas. After recovering from World War II, many countries made progressively heavier investments in science and education. Germany devoted large sums of money to basic and applied research. As we detailed earlier, Japan, South Korea, and Taiwan have made numerous targeted investments in specific technological capabilities in the 1960s, 1970s, 1980s, and 1990s, and these brought about dramatic changes in their relative global competitiveness.

Although delayed by the Cultural Revolution, China eventually launched some of the most ambitious efforts, both in scale and scope. Its "863" program, also known as the State High-Tech Development Plan, targeted the acquisition of specific capabilities that the country's leaders thought would free it from a dependence on foreign technology. The program initially sought to boost the innovation capacity of the country in strategic high-tech fields: biotechnology and advanced agricultural technology, information technology, advanced materials technology, advanced manufacturing and automation technology, and energy technology as well as resource and environmental technology.[24] Telecommunication and marine technology were subsequently added.

In 1997, China's State Science and Education Steering Group launched the National Plan on Key Basic Research and Development and the National Program on Key Basic Research Project (973 Program). The purpose of these two initiatives was to strengthen basic scientific research. The nation has followed with regular refreshes of its five-year plans, including the most recent, the Twelfth Five-Year Plan, which includes thirty-five projects to develop seven strategic emerging industries.[25] These projects include high-efficiency energy-saving technologies such as lighting; next-generation mobile communications; Internet core equipment, Internet of things, cloud computing, and high-end software and servers; biopharmaceuticals; high-end assembly and manufacturing, including aerospace, rail and transport, and smart assembly; nuclear, solar, wind, and biomass power and smart grids; advanced materials and composites; and electric and fuel-cell cars. The plan serves as a road map for government funding of research at universities and research institutes, the strategies of state-owned enterprises (SOEs), and specific projects, policies, and incentives. An example of such a policy was a grant for half of the purchase price of MOCVD (metal-organic chemical vapor deposition) tools that are used in the production of LEDs. A similar program several years ago was aimed at reducing the country's dependence on overseas suppliers of crystalline polysilicon, used in solar cells. Such actions help to ensure that China will become the global production center for these items.

Government Policy: A Failure to Keep Up with the New World

Once upon a time, US policy makers could comfortably assume that the United States had an unchallenged position in most science- and technology-based manufacturing industries. Over the past few decades, however, that assumption has looked increasingly tenuous and, in some cases, outright dated. The world has become a much more competitive place. Everyone wants to compete in the technology arena. With fewer restrictions on the flow of capital and goods, it has never been easier for companies to locate their operations wherever they think they can profit from the market dynamics. Fast-growing overseas markets are enticing American companies to move operations outside the United States.

US policies have not kept pace with this new reality. Too often, Washington has been reactive and has focused on symptoms rather than the causes of the disease, and has made policies without taking into account the broader consequences. Consider how the government responded when particular industries such as steel, semiconductors, and automobiles encountered serious foreign competition and suffered major declines. Government did step in to provide help in the form of import restriction or voluntary price restraints (under the rubric of "orderly market agreements"). Ultimately, in the case of GM and Chrysler, it provided bailouts. But the root causes—declining technical and manufacturing competitiveness (and, in the case of steel and autos, poor labor relations)—had been decades in the making.

Government investments in the commons reflect this lack of proactive, coherent thinking. As we noted earlier, the US government has historically played a central role in supporting the country's scientific and technological foundations. But is the government's commitment to scientific research still there? There are some worrisome signs that it is faltering. Whereas government support of basic scientific research grew steadily for several decades from the 1950s through the 1990s, it began to flatten around 2003 (figure 5-3).

Even more worrisome is how this funding has been allocated between basic and applied (sometimes called "use-inspired") research. Basic research typically covers work aimed at seeking to deepen understanding of first principles such as the genetic mechanisms that regulate how cancer cells grow. Applied research seeks to use that knowledge to answer more specific questions about a real-world problem, such as which particular genes are involved in

FIGURE 5-3

US federal government spending on basic and applied research (in billions of constant 2000 dollars)

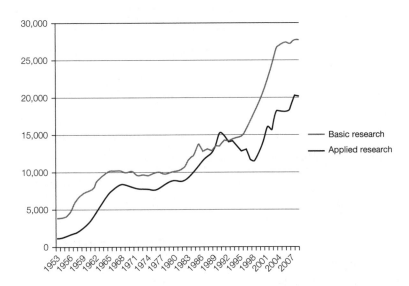

Source: National Science Board, *National Science and Engineering Indicators 2010* (Arlington, VA: National Science Foundation, 2010).

cancer. As shown in figure 5-3, government support for research was historically split pretty evenly between basic and applied research, reflecting their equal importance. However, since 1990, that has no longer been the case. Government spending for applied research declined 40 percent from 1990 to 1998. Although it rebounded sharply after 1998, it still lags well behind basic research.

We acknowledge that the distinction between basic and applied research is blurry in practice and in the accounting of the spending. Still, the picture is concerning. Because applied research acts as a bridge between pure science and commercial development, it is critical for innovation. Shortchanging applied research increases the odds that the fruits of US science will go unexploited in America.

There have also been significant shifts in the makeup of federal support for R&D, with a pronounced move toward spending a greater share on the life sciences and a smaller share on physical sciences and engineering. The National Science Foundation reported that while federal funding for R&D has more than doubled over twenty years (not adjusting for inflation), the proportion allocated to life sciences rose from 40 percent of the total to around half.[26] This trend is apparent in the data in figure 5-4 on spending for university research.

Thus, although the US government has been heavily supporting some parts of the commons (that related to medical sciences and biology), its support for others (such as physical sciences and computer sciences) has clearly not kept pace.

Business: Not Minding the Commons?

To understand what role businesses may be playing in the erosion of the industrial commons, we analyzed data over time on the R&D spending and capital investments of a sample of the largest American corporations. Why did we choose these two variables? R&D is clearly important because it is critical for innovation. It is

FIGURE 5-4

Academic R&D spending by field (in billions of constant 2000 dollars)

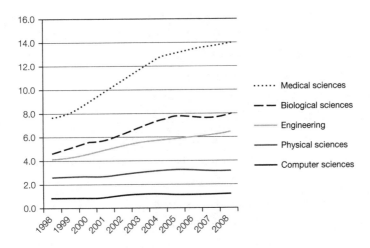

Medical sciences
Biological sciences
Engineering
Physical sciences
Computer sciences

Source: Data from National Science Board, *Science and Engineering Indicators 2010* (Arlington, VA: National Science Foundation, 2010).

also important because it tends to have large *spillovers* (economic benefits not fully captured by the investor). Capital investment is of interest because it drives productivity, which drives wages. It is also a critical foundation for the manufacturing component of the industrial commons. So by tracking R&D and capital investment, we can obtain a picture of how well businesses are "watering" the commons.

To gain a point of reference for R&D and capital investment, we also tracked how much the same companies were paying out to their investors in the forms of dividends and stock buybacks. The comparison of R&D, capital expenditures, and dividend/stock buybacks provides a picture of how American companies were prioritizing competing uses of their free cash flows.

The time frame for our analysis is 1980 to 2010. Our sample was created as follows: We started with the largest 1,000 companies by market capitalization in each of those years. We then eliminated companies that did not report R&D spending and further filtered the sample to include only companies from manufacturing industries. By limiting the sample to firms from manufacturing industries, we do not have to worry that changes in the mix of service and manufacturing companies in the sample are confounding the picture of total R&D spending (e.g., if service firms that don't spend much on R&D became more prevalent in the top 1,000 over time, it might appear that American firms were cutting back on their R&D spending). Depending on the year, there are between 300 and 500 firms in the sample, representing a substantial chunk of the total R&D spent by American companies.

The results of our analysis are shown in figure 5-5. We combine dividends and stock buybacks for visual clarity. One caveat: Data

FIGURE 5-5

US corporate spending on R&D, capital expenditures, and dividend plus stock buybacks (in billions of dollars)

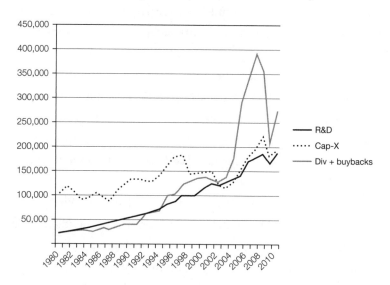

Source: Authors' analysis of Compustat data.

on stock buybacks for our sample was not available until 1992, so the "dividend + buybacks" figures prior to that date are really only dividends. However, because stock buybacks were relatively small prior to 1990, their exclusion likely has little impact on the overall trends.[27]

Two trends are striking in this data. The first is the surge in payouts to current shareholders relative to investments in R&D and capital expenditures. From 1980 to 2001, payouts to current shareholders via dividends and repurchases were about equal to investments in R&D. So in many ways, we could think about companies as investing $1 in potential future earnings (through R&D) for every $1 they gave back to shareholders. In the 2000s, however, the picture changes dramatically, with a payout surge (driven mostly by stock buybacks) dwarfing investments in R&D and capital expenditures. In the past decade, companies were choosing to give a much bigger chunk of their free cash flows to current shareholders than reinvesting them in R&D or capital expenditures.

The second notable trend is the relative stagnation in capital expenditures since the mid-1990s. Consider the following. Between 1992 and 2010, total R&D spending increased by 186 percent, whereas dividends and stock buybacks increased by 341 percent (buybacks alone increased 777 percent). But capital expenditures increased by only 50 percent. And, of course, stock buybacks were pummeled by the financial crisis. If we look at the data through 2008, the picture is even more striking. Whereas R&D increased by 186 percent from 1992 to 2008 and capital expenditures increased by 71 percent, dividends and buybacks increased by 472 percent.

In some ways, American companies (and America) experienced a "lost decade" of declining capital investment between 1997 and 2007. What is concerning is that this lack of investment can in no way be attributable to a lack of capital. During those ten years, the companies in our sample spent about $2.1 *trillion* on dividends and stock buybacks. It was clearly a good time to be an investor (or an executive compensated with stock options). But the manufacturing component of the industrial commons eroded.

Moreover, because this data includes companies' *global* expenditures (i.e., the investments in or R&D spending of their foreign affiliates), it does not tell the full story. The picture gets even more worrisome when we consider that for the past few decades, US companies have been increasing their capital and R&D investments in their overseas subsidiaries at a much faster rate than in their domestic US operations. According to data compiled by the Bureau of Economic Analysis (BEA), in 1989, capital expenditures made by US multinationals' foreign affiliates accounted for 22 percent of their total global capital expenditures; by 2009, this share had increased to 29 percent. The same picture emerges for R&D. In 1989, R&D spending of US multinationals' foreign affiliates accounted for only 8.8 percent of these companies' total R&D spending; by 2009, R&D spending at foreign affiliates had increased to 15.6 percent.[28]

Because the sample in our analysis excludes foreign companies operating in the United States, we could be underestimating investment in the American commons. After all, many foreign companies (e.g., Toyota, BMW) build plants in the United States. To address this issue, we analyzed BEA data that includes all companies operating in the United States.

Another advantage of the BEA data is that it allows us to dissect expenditures more finely and identify two types of capital investments most closely associated with manufacturing: investments in manufacturing structures (such as plant buildings) and investments in industrial equipment. We also included R&D spending as a point of comparison. To make the comparison easier to visualize in figure 5-6, we indexed the numbers so that 2005 equals 100 for expenditures on manufacturing structures, expenditures on industrial equipment, and R&D investment (thus, the intersection of the

FIGURE 5-6

US investments in manufacturing structures, industrial equipment, and R&D (index: 2005 = 100)

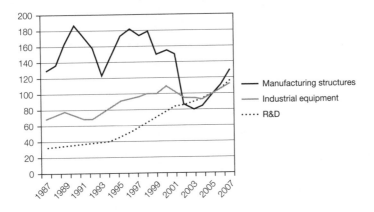

Source: Authors' analysis of data from the Bureau of Economic Analysis.

lines does not mean that the spending was the same). This approach makes sense given that we are most interested in the relative rates of change, rather than the absolute expenditures.

This analysis revealed that investment in manufacturing structures (e.g., new plants) has actually declined overall since the late 1980s. Investment in industrial equipment increased, but at a significantly slower rate than spending on R&D. The trends in this more expansive data set are consistent with the move away from hard assets revealed in our earlier analysis.

Management Behaviors Behind These Trends

Decisions to invest in R&D or capital expenditures (and whether to do so at home or abroad) are made by managers. At one level, these decisions are guided by analytical models (the cold calculus of net present value and financial returns taught in business schools). At another level, however, they are shaped by underlying management philosophies. After all, as any manager will attest, the analytical models at their disposal have their limits. For complex decisions, judgment matters. Two key features of management philosophy over the past few decades help to explain the trends observed above. The first is the notion that hard assets are less valuable than intangible assets (we call this "the flight from hard assets"). The second is a presumption that it is always better to buy rather than build.

THE FLIGHT FROM HARD ASSETS

The notion that hard assets such as manufacturing plants and equipment no longer matter to competitive advantage in knowledge-based industries has come to pervade American management thinking. Indeed, the philosophy has been that these assets should be minimized. They are a drain on the income statement (through depreciation) and are an albatross around the neck of the balance sheet. As we have argued earlier, we think this philosophy is misguided. The flight from hard assets resulting from this philosophy is often just the first step in a process of flight from *hard skills* such as engineering design, process development, equipment development, and process improvement. Those skills are so intimately connected to the hard assets that where the assets go, so go the skills.

Too many companies now accept this philosophy. There are exceptions. No one would doubt that Intel has been on the forefront of the knowledge economy. Its microprocessors power the information revolution. Furthermore, no one would doubt the company's credentials as a serious knowledge creator. In 2010, it spent $5.5 billion on R&D. Yet the company is not afraid to invest in the hard assets needed to capture value from its R&D investment. Intel has bucked traditional wisdom in the semiconductor industry by maintaining a vertical integration strategy in manufacturing. In 2010, it invested $5.2 billion on capital expenditures (the vast majority of which went to manufacturing plants).

Corning is another exception. The 160-year-old company headquartered in upstate New York has been at the leading edge of technical innovation in glass, ceramics, and advanced materials. In 2010, it invested $600 million in R&D (about 10 percent of sales) but also invested about $1 billion in capital expenditures. Like Intel, Corning's process capabilities represent a *hard skill* that keep it at the leading edge and ahead of competitors.

BUYING VERSUS BUILDING

Being a procurement manager now is a bit like being a kid in candy store—a very big candy store. You have choices like never before. Need electronics assembly? You can find great low-cost suppliers in China, Asia, and Mexico. Need software services? India is the best-known place to go, but the quality-to-cost equation is also outstanding in eastern Europe. Need chemical development and manufacturing? China, Korea, India, and eastern Europe offer a lot of great choices.

For the past few decades, as the global economy has opened, companies have been taught about the virtues of staying flexible and avoiding commitments of assets to specific locations. Once you build a plant, this line of thinking goes, it's stuck there. Let someone else do it, and then buy from them. If a better option becomes available next year, take it. Why commit to your workforce when you might find a better deal sourcing from another part of the world next year?

Multinationals have done a great job utilizing the global markets for products and labor, and essentially exploiting arbitrage opportunities. As Michael Spence and Sandile Hlatshwayo point out, multinational sourcing has improved the efficiency of the global market for goods and service.[29] We concur 100 percent with their assessment. However, we question whether companies have gone too far in seeking to exploit market failures and arbitrage opportunities by rapidly shifting sourcing rather than trying to create unique capabilities in the locations where they operate. Companies may be helping to make markets more efficient, but will the companies that pursue such an approach ultimately be more profitable over the long run?

We think that companies that do not make commitments to local industrial commons and local communities run a risk. In economic theory, commitment is a dual-edged sword. On the one hand, it locks you in and limits options. The arbitrage model of sourcing is based on the idea of avoiding commitment as much as possible so that you have options.

On the other hand, your company clearly may also benefit when others—such as workers, suppliers, customers, collaborators, and so on—make long-term commitments to your organization. For instance, a worker who engages in specialized training that makes him or her more productive in your factory is making a commitment that helps your organization. A supplier that decides to build its factory right next to yours to reduce transportation costs and improve coordination is making a commitment that benefits your organization.

We like it when others make specialized commitments to us. We benefit. But can we realistically expect workers, suppliers, customers, and other partners to make commitments to us if we do not make commitments to them? Economic theory (and common sense) is quite clear on the answer: absolutely not. If you won't commit to your suppliers, your suppliers are unlikely to make specialized investments that increase their commitments to you. They are not fools! In pursuing the buy/arbitrage strategy of sourcing, companies have made an implicit, and not always wise, trade-off. By not making commitments, they have gained the efficiency that comes from the flexibility to source wherever costs are lowest. At the same time, by not making commitments, they have lost the efficiencies that come when partners make specialized investments.

The rise of the American industrial commons was neither natural nor inevitable. It was the product of both government and private enterprises exploiting circumstances. In the same vein, the decline of the American industrial commons is neither natural nor inevitable. Yes, the circumstances have changed dramatically. The United States faces a far more challenging and complex world economy. But that does not mean decline is inevitable. In the final two chapters of this book, we examine what both businesses and government need to be doing to reverse this decline.

CHAPTER 6

Rebuilding the Commons

The Visible Hand of Management

Business leadership matters. No economy can succeed without an ample supply of talented, well-trained, and motivated managers. Indeed, business historian Alfred Chandler says that one of the main reasons for the rise of the American economy in the late nineteenth and early twentieth centuries was the emergence of a professional "managerial class." In the latter part of the twentieth century, American entrepreneurs transformed the economy by driving the creation and growth of the semiconductor, personal computer, software, biotechnology, and computer graphics industries, as well as e-commerce and the Internet. This chapter is about the role managers can and should play in the twenty-first century to rejuvenate the American industrial commons.

We're sure that plenty of people will react negatively to this call and will argue that it's unfair to ask managers of private enterprises to add one more thing to their agendas. They already have their hands full dealing with aggressive competitors, tough markets, and incessant investor pressures.

There are also plenty of economists and executives who will contend that it is unrealistic to expect multinationals to put country before company. They will note that although the headquarters of "American" multinationals are in the United States, their shareholders come from around the world, they may employ more people outside than inside the United States, other countries are probably generating a large and rapidly growing share of their revenues, and people who are neither American citizens nor American residents are increasingly filling their management ranks. At a symposium on US competitiveness that Harvard Business School held in November 2011, the CEO of a prominent American corporation reflected the identity crisis that leaders of American multinationals are having when he said, "As an American, I am rooting for the American economy, but half my management team are not Americans, and more than half my employees work outside the U.S. So for me to tell them as CEO that I want to do something good for America is not necessarily a message they are going to be all that excited about."

Our response to all this is that it is both business's and government's responsibility to rebuild the American industrial commons. (We'll examine what the government can and should do to rebuild the commons in the next chapter.) Let us be clear: we're not calling for business leaders to do so in order to be patriotic or to fulfill some sort of civic duty. Rather, we believe that it is often in a company's long-term interest to invest in and support the local industrial commons in which it operates.

There is nothing wrong with globalizing operations. Indeed, it is imperative for many companies. But all too often, companies have lost sight of the strategic value of their local industrial commons and have recklessly reduced their presence in them or abandoned them. Taking actions that might weaken an industrial commons in which a company has been a long-time participant can be risky, because a strong commons provides its members with a potent competitive advantage. Thus, doing anything that weakens a commons harms not only the economy of the country where that commons resides but the company as well.

If some executives don't buy this logic, it is undoubtedly because they subscribe to a type of management, or leadership, that is all too prevalent today—one that sees market and competitor analysis alone as the key to formulating strategy, that views manufacturing as a cost, and that thinks that catering to the short-term interest of shareholders is the leadership priority. In contrast, we argue that strong leadership involves recognizing the following:

- Superior capabilities that reside in a commons are a precious source of competitive advantage and therefore are integral to strategy.

- The value of a healthy industrial commons and the close proximity of R&D and manufacturing should be factored into decisions about whether to outsource an operation or to invest in building or improving it.

- Leaders should act in the long-term interest of the enterprise and all its stakeholders and not in the short-term interest of a particular set of shareholders.

Let's examine these elements in greater depth.

A New Mind-Set: Competing Through Capabilities

If you are a sports fan, you know that the team that usually wins any competition is the one with the better overall capabilities (a combination of raw talent, attitude, and the capacity to work in synch). In military conflicts, capabilities—rooted in a combination of weaponry, training, motivation, and tactical skills—can trump sheer size of force. In business, companies such as Apple, BMW,

IBM, GE, Intel, Taiwan Semiconductor, Corning, Southwest Airlines, and Toyota have sustained advantages by possessing capabilities their competitors just cannot seem to match. As we pointed out in the last chapter, many companies have fallen prey to a "buy rather than build" mentality. Rather than creating proprietary capabilities themselves, they seek advantage by doing a better job of procuring them from others. This mentality runs directly counter to the capabilities-based approach to competition that we advocate. After all, if you can buy something (e.g., access to low-cost labor) from a third-party provider, so can your competitors. There is no differentiation—no strategic value—in being able to do things *as well as* your competitors. Competitive advantage accrues only to those enterprises that have developed unique, difficult-to-imitate capabilities.[1]

Viewing capabilities as *the* source of a company's competitive advantage has direct implications for how one thinks about investments in the industrial commons. A company that competes this way is always on the lookout for an edge in creating or gaining privileged access to skills and know-how. It realizes that such capabilities are built up over long periods of time and often have a location-specific character, because the skills, know-how, and capabilities built up by workers, suppliers, and other partners in a local industrial commons may be hard to replicate elsewhere. Deep relationships—knowing how to work effectively with other members of the commons and a mutual trust that can only be built up over time—are another important asset that simply cannot be procured elsewhere. Again, this is *not* an argument against branching out to new locations or cultivating new relationships with new workforces and suppliers; we're simply saying that companies should not ignore or minimize the value of the capabilities they have already created in their existing commons. That value should be incorporated into decisions about whether to invest in or outsource activities such as R&D and manufacturing and where to locate those operations. We'll discuss how to do so later in the chapter.

There are a number of practical steps managers can take to turn their companies into capabilities-advantaged competitors:

- *Make building capabilities an explicit goal in the strategy process.* Strategy is an answer to a simple question: How do we intend to win? There are various components of this question. One is, What game do we intend to play? This component, which concerns choices of product markets and positions within the selected markets, often receives the lion's share of attention in strategy-making processes and involves traditional techniques such as market and competitor analysis. It also tends to be the more visible part of strategic battles: everyone can observe how well different competitors are doing in the market for mobile communication devices, cars, computers, and so on.

    The more difficult part of strategy making concerns answering this question: What unique skills or capabilities do we need in order to win at our chosen game? We have found that many companies don't give this question anywhere close to the consideration it deserves. This is largely because the traditional analytical apparatus of management is not well suited to this question. For example, traditional net-present-value analysis will tell you pretty clearly the costs of creating a capability (investment in R&D, capital expenditure, workforce training, etc.), but it won't tell you the costs of having that capability flow to competitors if you choose to outsource it.

- *Include executives with deep knowledge of capabilities in the strategy-making process.* This means senior executives with intimate knowledge of the company's technology, operating processes, culture on the shop floor, and supplier network. A strategy process run largely as a financial exercise and dominated by executives with little in-depth knowledge of the company's technology and operations is unlikely to place much emphasis on how capabilities can create advantage.

- *Take a dynamic perspective.* The most strategically valuable capabilities—those that are the hardest to imitate—take the longest to create. They are built not in a one-year crash R&D or capital-expenditure binge. Rather, they are the result of cumulative investments in both physical and human capital made over years, which, of course, requires deep, sustained commitment.[2]

Companies with this mind-set assume that competitors will not sit still and, therefore, are constantly looking for ways to deepen or expand their capabilities. Their executives understand that, like muscles, capabilities atrophy without use and often cannot be easily rehabilitated once they have withered. Indeed a decision to *not* invest in continuing to build a capability or to close a plant and outsource manufacturing to an off-shore supplier is an irreversible decision. Dell and Hewlett-Packard learned this the hard way. They didn't realize that when they chose to let third parties design and manufacture their personal computers, they were giving up their ability to compete as innovators. Now they are paying the price and have to play catch-up to Apple in the fast-growing tablet market.

Taking a dynamic perspective also means recognizing that a cost structure is never fixed by time or place. Many companies operating plants in high-cost places such as the United States and western Europe have too quickly assumed that those locations were inherently uncompetitive due to higher wages and higher prices for other things (e.g., land, required pollution-control equipment, and electricity) and have succumbed to the temptation to move production to lower-cost countries.

There are several things wrong with this thinking. As companies are discovering today with China (and as others learned decades ago in other parts of Asia), wages typically rise over time. What is a low-cost location today may not be a low-cost location tomorrow. In addition, a place that appears to be a high-cost site does not necessarily have to be so: investments in process R&D, workforce training, and other operating capabilities can generate significant productivity improvements that can offset cost differentials. Jan Rivkin and Michael Porter, our colleagues at Harvard, call this approach "improve, not move."[3]

- *Recognize that superior operating capabilities cannot be bought with investments in R&D or new factories alone.* Capabilities are rooted in a system of interdependent pieces. As mentioned in chapter 3, Toyota opened its factories to competitors eager to replicate the vaunted Toyota production system. Yet none has been able to fully imitate it. This is because capabilities like Toyota's are rooted in a complex, interdependent mix of decisions about how it designs its products, processes, and assembly lines; manages suppliers, quality, and inventory; schedules production; trains and motivates its workers; implements shop-floor improvement; and a host of other factors. This makes imitation hard. That's why these kinds of capabilities are so potent competitively.

The lesson is that capabilities require persistent attention and investments across all parts of the organization. As we will discuss in the next section, they can also benefit from being close to a healthy industrial commons.

Getting the Math Right on Location Decisions

In too many companies, decisions about where to locate manufacturing plants or to source products are made largely on the basis of narrow financial criteria. Manufacturing is viewed as a cost center, and the objective of the analysis is to minimize total costs.

Proposals to invest in manufacturing assets are treated like any other investment proposal and subject to strict return hurdles. Tax, regulatory, intellectual property, and political considerations also often figure heavily in the conversation.

However, these analyses rarely adequately take into account the value of operating in a healthy industrial commons and the impact of the company's decision on the health of the commons. To be more specific, they don't adequately consider how locating manufacturing far away from R&D would affect the company's ability to innovate and whether a decision to source more production from distant locations would harm a local industrial commons that is ultimately a potent long-term source of advantage. Undoubtedly, one reason these issues are excluded from the decision-making process is that they are difficult to quantify. But if you leave them out of the equation, the numbers will be misleading. Let's look at how to get the calculus right.

Understand the Strategic Value of Belonging to a Strong Industrial Commons

In an increasingly globalized world, location paradoxically matters more, not less, for companies because it can mean having privileged access to capabilities in a commons that can keep you ahead of competitors. Therefore, managers must fully understand the value of the capabilities provided by the commons in which their companies operate. This requires an in-depth assessment of supplier capabilities, workforce skills, the quality of local institutions (such as universities or vocational schools), and the sophistication and capabilities of customers, as well as an analysis of how being geographically proximate to these resources helps your own operations.

Does exploiting this "localness" mean not being global? Absolutely not. Although a US-based company should nurture and leverage industrial commons in America, it should also be thinking about how to exploit localness in other places around the world where it operates as well. Being global means building roots in multiple places throughout the world, not being rootless. Novartis, whose corporate headquarters are in Basel, Switzerland, has its research headquarters in Cambridge, Massachusetts (and has research operations in California, the United Kingdom, Switzerland, Italy, China, and Singapore). It chooses locations that offer fertile networks of talent and collaborators and attempts to immerse itself in the local ecosystems.

Similarly, when making sourcing or plant-location decisions, it's important to understand whether an option would hurt a strategically important commons. For example, if you are a large member of the commons—say, a dominant buyer or a critical supplier—then recognize that your decision to close a plant or change the sourcing of something from the commons to an offshore location could inflict a serious blow to the commons. Thus, you need to ask how the deterioration of the commons over time will affect your ability to access critical capabilities.

There is no easy way to quantify this impact. In some cases, the capabilities in a commons may have grown obsolete or irrelevant. In others, key partners (such as suppliers or workers) may have failed to upgrade their skills. In these situations, the commons may no longer be offering much of an advantage, and it may be time to move on.

The Impact of Innovation

As we have argued throughout this book, the integration of R&D and manufacturing is essential to innovation in many circumstances.[4] How can a company evaluate the costs of geographically separating R&D and manufacturing when making sourcing decisions? As explained in chapter 4, the cost depends on two factors. One is the ability of R&D and manufacturing to operate independently of each other—in other words, how *modular* the product and process technology are. The other is the *maturity* of the process—by which we mean how much a manufacturing process has evolved. We have included the manufacturing–modularity matrix here again for your reference (figure 6-1).

Our framework does not obviate the need for rigorous financial analysis of manufacturing investments. Nor does it override other considerations that might influence sourcing decisions, such as proximity to customers, political barriers to market entry, taxes, and regulations. Rather, it's designed to help managers think more strategically about the consequences of geographically separating R&D and manufacturing.

FIGURE 6-1

The modularity–maturity matrix

Process-embedded innovation	**Pure product innovation**
Process technologies, though mature, are still highly integral to product innovation. Subtle changes in process can alter the product's characteristics in unpredictable ways. *Design cannot be separated from manufacturing.* EXAMPLES Craft products, high-end wine, high-end apparel, heat-treated metal fabrication, advanced materials fabrication, specialty chemicals	The processes are mature, and the value of integrating product design with manufacturing is low. *Outsourcing manufacturing makes sense.* EXAMPLES Desktop computers, consumer electronics, active pharmaceutical ingredients, commodity semiconductors
Process-driven innovation	**Pure process innovation**
Major process innovations are evolving rapidly and can have a huge impact on the product. The value of integrating R&D and manufacturing is extremely high. *The risks of separating design and manufacturing are enormous.* EXAMPLES Biotech drugs, nano-materials, OLED and electrophoretic displays, superminiaturized assembly	Process technology is evolving rapidly but is not intimately connected to product innovation. *While locating product design near manufacturing is not critical, proximity between process R&D and manufacturing is.* EXAMPLES Advanced semiconductors, high-density flexible circuits

Vertical axis (low to high): **Process: maturity the degree to which the process has evolved**

Horizontal axis (low to high): **Modularity: the degree to which information about product design can be separated from the manufacturing process**

Source: Reprinted with permission from Gary P. Pisano and Willy C. Shih, "Does America Really Need Manufacturing?" *Harvard Business Review*, March 2012, 96.

To devise an appropriate manufacturing strategy, you have to determine which quadrant your business falls into. Although there is no simple formula that can tell you whether the manufacturing technology is mature and the product design and process technology are modular, there are some factors that can inform your judgment (table 6-1).

First, if a process technology hasn't changed in quite some time (or if the changes are largely incremental) and current performance (in terms of yields, quality, and costs) appears to meet the market's demands, your business is probably in a mature sector. If costs are

TABLE 6-1

The design-manufacturing relationship: what to ask

Assessing process maturity		Assessing modularity	
When was the last major change in basic process technology in your business?	How well do current process technologies meet commercial requirements (costs, yields, quality, and so on)?	To what extent are product-design choices constrained by process technology and manufacturing capabilities?	To what extent can a product design be described without referencing the manufacturing process?
What has the rate of change in process technology been over the past five years?	What is the likelihood that a major upheaval in process technology will occur in the next five years?	How much impact would a minor variation in the manufacturing process have on the product's crucial characteristics?	To what extent can the product design and process design be codified?
How much process R&D is being conducted by companies in your industry, including equipment vendors and other suppliers?		How well understood are the underlying relationships between product parameters and process parameters?	Are there standardized process platforms that are compatible with specific ranges of product designs?

Source: Reprinted with permission from Gary P. Pisano and Willy C. Shih, "Does America Really Need Manufacturing?" *Harvard Business Review*, March 2012, 98–99.

falling, yields are increasing dramatically, processes are changing rapidly, and you expect competitors or equipment vendors to continue to invest heavily in process R&D, your business is probably in an immature process sector. Talking to vendors and even to companies from other industries may help you identify whether significant process innovations are on the horizon.

Second, process parameters that are difficult to codify, process changes that significantly affect product characteristics, and a lack of standardized processes are all telltale signs of low modularity, but an in-depth discussion among product designers, process engineers, and manufacturing personnel is often needed. People from different functions can have very different perspectives on this issue. Product designers frequently underestimate the degree to which their design choices affect manufacturing processes. Likewise, process engineers and manufacturing personnel often do not realize how changes in a process or operation might affect a design.

In too many companies, the people who actually know the most about how manufacturing location decisions might influence innovation have no voice in these decisions. One biotechnology company we spoke with during our research decided, with virtually no input from its process-development scientists, to outsource production to a supplier halfway around the world. (The decision was made based strictly on an analysis of the capital costs and financial returns.) Even though the company used an experienced and competent overseas contractor, the contractor had problems scaling up production and improving yields. Serious supply shortages ensued, which damaged the company's stock price. Ultimately, the firm was acquired.

When using these guidelines, it is important to consider not only where things stand today but also where they're going, which tends to be a lot more difficult because technologies do not always evolve in predictable ways. In assessing trends, keep the following precepts in mind.

MANUFACTURING TECHNOLOGIES CAN BE REJUVENATED

There is a tendency to view any given process-technology life cycle as a one-way street, from infancy to maturity (like our own human life cycle). When a company operates in a sector in which the process technology is mature, it's tempting to dismiss the possibility of process innovation and seek to reduce costs by outsourcing or moving production to lower-cost offshore environments. But game-changing process technologies sometimes can emerge.

For many decades the steel industry was viewed as a classic mature process-technology business, and many large steel manufacturers in the United States and Europe had pretty much given up on process innovation. They focused on rationalizing capacity and moving production to lower-cost locations. Then in the 1970s, mini-mills that employed electric arc furnaces and other novel process technologies ushered in a renaissance in the steel industry that left many mature players in ruins. Similarly, a new molding technology that dramatically reduced the costs and improved the consistency of contact-lens production enabled Johnson & Johnson to turn the contact lens market on its head through the introduction of disposable contact lenses. The established players that were busy incrementally refining their existing technologies for making conventional lenses were caught off-guard and saw their market shares plummet.

A similar rebirth occurred in the consumer electronics industry. In the 1960s and 1970s, many people in industry believed that the product and manufacturing technologies were at the tail end of their life cycles. Making televisions, stereo equipment, and radios was then a labor-intensive process that required little skill or sophistication and could be performed just about anywhere. This led US consumer electronics giants to move production to low-cost offshore locations. Over the next two decades, however, radically new product and process technologies were introduced.

Today, manufacturing consumer electronics involves highly sophisticated, leading-edge process technologies, high-density packaging, advanced displays, and sophisticated energy-storage and management technologies.

BEWARE OF "DEMODULARIZATION"

Sometimes new technologies can also make product-design and manufacturing processes much more interdependent. Consider jetliners. For decades their design and manufacture were highly modular. That explains why Boeing could outsource major chunks of its aircraft development and manufacturing to subcontractors around the world and then assemble the planes in its factories in the state of Washington. But in the 787 Dreamliner program, the shift from aluminum alloys to carbon-fiber-composite materials changed things. The old modular design rules could not fully account for stress transmission and loading at the system level—something that Boeing did not get right initially. As a result, it encountered problems assembling pieces (such as the horizontal stabilizer from Alenia Aeronautica in Italy and the side of body wing join). Significant redesign and rework were required, and the program suffered major delays.

DO NOT SQUANDER AN ADVANTAGE CREATED BY LOW MODULARITY

Many companies fail to recognize that the deep integration of their product-design and manufacturing processes is actually a major source of competitive advantage. It poses a major barrier to entry for newcomers, who must master the product technology, the process technology, and the interactions between the two. Therefore, when R&D-manufacturing modularity is low, incumbents shouldn't outsource production.

It is generally much easier to reverse-engineer a product design than to figure out someone else's proprietary manufacturing process. This helps to explain why companies in the fashion apparel business such as Zegna, Armani, Ferragamo, and MaxMara keep the bulk of their high-end production in Italy despite the high costs. In this part of the industry, the link between product design and manufacturing is very tight. How a fabric is cut or how a seam is sewn, for instance, can affect the way a garment drapes in subtle ways that matter. By keeping production close to home, these companies can better protect their proprietary design and reduce the risk of imitation. For similar reasons, GE Aviation keeps the manufacture of key components of its jet engines as well as the assembly process—both of which rely on tight integration between design and manufacturing—close to home.

Some companies, though, have inadvertently undermined their own low-modularity advantage by outsourcing production. We see this happening today in biotechnology. Because biotech plants are capital intensive, some companies are outsourcing manufacturing to third parties and training them to do it. Aside from the point we made earlier—that this is vastly easier said than done, especially for new products—this strategy runs the risk of diffusing proprietary know-how, making processes more standardized across the industry and dramatically reducing the role manufacturing can play as a barrier to entry. As "bio-similars" (essentially generic versions of biotechnology drugs) come into greater use in the future, the loss of this manufacturing advantage could be something innovative biotech firms come to regret.

Leadership Matters

We often hear that the approach we advocate is simply not practical given the intense pressures senior executives face to optimize the share price of their companies in the short term. "The stock market only cares about what we do next quarter. We just do not have the time to invest for the long term," many executives say. We call this "the devil made me do it" excuse for poor leadership.

There is no evidence that the stock market reacts poorly to companies that invest for the long term. Consider the biotechnology industry. Total industry profits of all publicly held biotechnology companies have been negative for most years of the industry's life (going back to the mid-1970s). Many biotechnology companies have never earned a profit (even after more than a decade in business).[5] And yet, the biotechnology industry has received hundreds of billions of dollars in public equity investment since its inception. If stock markets were so short sighted, we would not see industries such as biotechnology and pharmaceuticals and a company such as Boeing, which has to invest more than $10 billion over more than a decade to create a new-generation aircraft.

There are three impediments to pursuing long-term strategies built around capabilities:

- *The design of executive compensation systems.* Over the past few decades, companies (or more specifically, their boards of directors) have increasingly tied executive compensation to the performance of the company's stock price. In an article in *Harvard Business Review*, our Harvard colleague Mihir Desai refers to this as "outsourcing" the decision about executive compensation to the financial markets.[6] If managers are under the impression that stock markets are short sighted (rightly or wrongly), then compensation packages heavily based on stock-market returns will have a predictable impact on their behavior. Clearly, this is a failure of the boards that set compensation policies. They need to utilize incentive compensation schemes that emphasize long-term value creation (e.g., restricted stock and long-term vesting and metrics tied to long-term value creation).

- *Technology- and operations-savvy boards.* If we expect boards to evaluate CEO performance (rather than outsourcing it to financial markets) and to evaluate long-term technology and operations strategies, then we need boards that are as comfortable with technology and operations as they are with finance, accounting, and marketing. This means changing the makeup of boards. Currently, there is an abundance of lawyers, accountants, bankers, and CEOs from other companies on boards, including those of many high-technology companies. However, scientists are shockingly rare, and manufacturing experts are even harder to find on boards. Yes, many companies have some type of "science and technology advisory board," but these groups typically wield little influence, and they certainly lack the fiduciary teeth of board committees. Hardly any companies have a board committee that focuses on technology and manufacturing issues. If a company's long-term competitive advantage depends on it making wise investments in manufacturing and technology, why not have a board committee (not an advisory committee) focused on these issues?

- *Management by numbers.* Managing for the long term is harder than managing for the short term. Optimizing next year's earnings is much easier than trying to understand where technologies are headed in five years or longer. Existing management techniques—those still stressed by business schools—focus on things that can be measured precisely, and it's much easier to measure precisely those things whose outcomes don't stretch way into the future. Many managers feel a lot more secure relying on numerical estimates and complex calculation in making decisions. (Sadly, their training at business schools helped make them that way.) Making commitments to technologies and building capabilities, as we have discussed, often forces executives to venture beyond their comfort zones. Again, we're not suggesting that executives *not* employ modern quantitative tools. Rigorous financial analysis is very important. But so is good old-fashioned judgment. Great business leaders need to engage in both digital and analog thinking.

Some of the strategies we have discussed in this chapter fly in the face of what has become conventional wisdom in the business and investment communities. Following our suggestions will take some courage. A manager who decides to rejuvenate a local plant in the United States rather than to shut it and move production to Asia risks being attacked for "being unwilling to make the tough decision." Inevitably, some analyst on Wall Street will write a damning report about how the CEO is mismanaging the company. Its stock price may drop. The CEO's board might start grumbling. This is not easy stuff. That's why so few companies actually do it. But that is precisely why it is so valuable. It's great leadership.

Conclusion

Our suggestions in this chapter are designed to help managers make their companies more fit to thrive over the long run in an increasingly competitive world. Under some circumstances, the commons and a firm's manufacturing capabilities are a potent source of value. They enable a firm to innovate and grow. This is not always the case, so this is by no means a blanket call to "in-source." This is about making investments and commitments that ultimately pay off in terms of giving a company a location-based advantage.

This chapter, however, only tells half the story. Making the commons an attractive locus of investment depends on many factors beyond an individual company's control, such as the education of the workforce, the creation of a modern infrastructure, and the supply of intellectual capital and know-how. We tackle these issues in our next chapter on government policy.

CHAPTER 7

Toward a National Economic Strategy for Manufacturing

All too often, the debate about what role Washington should play in supporting innovation degenerates into a battle between two extremes: the laissez-faire free-market camp and advocates of centralized industrial policy. Advocates of the free market see most government intervention as misguided, ineffective, or even worse, destructive. If manufacturing is declining, so be it; that's the market at work and the market knows best. At the other extreme are the advocates of industrial policy who see markets as inherently flawed and look to the government to set things right. In their view, businesses (and managers) are just too focused on their own short-term interests to make the investments that benefit the country over the long term.

Listening to both sides, you'd think there is no middle ground: it is *either* market *or* government. But as demonstrated in chapter 5, history says otherwise. Although the United States has perhaps the most market-oriented economy in the world, federal and, to a lesser extent, state governments have long played a central role in supporting technological innovation. But they did so in concert with market forces. That is, government policies if effectively designed can work as a *complement* to, not substitute for, market forces. In this chapter, we describe what such effective policies for helping rebuild the American industrial commons might look like.

There are, of course, many potential policy levers and options that the United States might use to restore its industrial commons as a way to support innovation: education, tax policies, government support of research, training, antitrust policies, subsidies, intellectual property policies, trade policies, procurement, and regulations. Policy debates concerning manufacturing often focus on one particular lever or the other. For instance, in 2008, there was a lot of debate about whether the federal government should have bailed out GM and Chrysler. This year (2012), there is a lot of debate on tax policy (President Obama recently announced that he wants to cut the maximum corporate tax rate to 28 percent and 25 percent for companies that manufacture). Trade policy—particularly with respect to China—rears its head regularly. What's lacking in discussion of policy concerning manufacturing is a comprehensive framework that considers the overall goal and how the various component policies fit together. In essence, we need a national economic strategy for manufacturing.[1]

A strategy is nothing more than a commitment to a set of priorities and pattern of action intended to achieve some objective. Strategy, by definition, involves trade-offs.[2] Most important, strategy is not only about what you will do, but also about what you will *not* do. When applied to American manufacturing, a national economic strategy must make clear our objectives and our priorities. It must highlight the kinds of policy interventions we will emphasize, and those we will take off the table.

The Objectives of a Strategy for Manufacturing

The very first question about the objectives of the manufacturing component of a national economic strategy is: What is the country hoping to achieve? There could be various objectives for a manufacturing strategy: maximizing the number of high-wage jobs, improving overall productivity, expanding the total number of jobs available for people without college educations, maximizing exports, and so on. Objectives such as these are often mentioned as the rationale behind various policy interventions that target manufacturing. For instance, President Obama has been very clear that preserving and creating jobs is the goal of his implemented and proposed policies to support American manufacturing. Because jobs affect elections, it is easy to understand why politicians emphasize them. However, job creation is not a compelling reason for a national manufacturing strategy. Manufacturing now accounts for only about one in ten American jobs. With increasing productivity (again, a healthy thing), it is hard to imagine how manufacturing could ever return to the days when it employed about a quarter of the US workforce. Instead of job creation, we believe that the central objective of a national manufacturing strategy should be keeping America's innovation capabilities healthy, because innovation drives productivity and productivity drives wages.

It follows that government policies should focus only on two types of manufacturing capabilities. These are the kinds that we identified in chapter 4: those pertaining to immature, or newly emerging, process technologies and those in contexts in which manufacturing-process innovation is highly interdependent with product R&D. In both cases, the manufacturing capabilities need to be geographically close to R&D.

Conversely, the national strategy should explicitly acknowledge that the United States cannot excel at all types of manufacturing and should not try to do so. The manufacturing that should not receive government support includes the kinds that are highly labor intensive or require relatively low-skilled workers. These are not the kinds of manufacturing that will drive productivity or innovation in the United States and are best left to emerging economies.

The notion that US policy should focus on certain kinds of manufacturing may strike some readers as dangerously close to *targeting* or *picking winners*—words often associated with "industrial policy." But we see a big difference between the government supporting certain classes of manufacturing *capabilities* and the government targeting support for specific manufacturing industries. A strategy for manufacturing has to be clear about which kind of interventions should and should not be used.

The Wrong Interventions

History teaches us that targeted attempts by government to support specific industries are rarely effective.[3] Such attempts can take a variety of forms, including tax breaks, loans or loan guarantees, and even direct intervention in restructuring an industry around a few chosen "national champions." There is a long history of such policies in the United States, Europe, and Japan, and the track record across countries is generally poor. European governments, for instance, tried in vain for decades to build a strong semiconductor industry by offering targeted subsidies to designated national champions.[4] In the 1960s, the United States heavily subsidized the development of a commercial supersonic transport jetliner—largely in response to European government programs that did the same— but none of these efforts resulted in a commercially successful plane.[5] The synthetic fuels program of the late 1970s and 1980s, which created a government-funded corporation to develop commercial plants for making alternatives to imported fossil fuels, is another case of failed targeting. The most recent example is federal and state loans and subsidies to solar-panel companies such as Solyndra and Evergreen Solar that either failed or closed their US operations. Even Japan's once-vaunted MITI has a checkered past. It gets credit for spawning Japan's semiconductor industry but almost wrecked its auto industry.

In general, governments do a lousy job playing venture capitalist or banker. Picking projects that are likely to be commercially successful or picking companies that are likely to excel requires deep insights into market dynamics, competitive conditions, and customer needs that government agencies lack. And of course, once these kinds of resource-allocation decisions are in the hands of government, they become subject to all the usual distortions of the political process, such as pressures from special interest groups and political constituencies. No one should be surprised that such interventions rarely make sense economically.

No one says that private enterprises and venture capitalists get it right every time. However, the virtue of markets is diversification and the law of large numbers. Markets create hundreds of parallel experiments. Given the ex ante uncertainty of innovation, markets are a highly effective mechanism for sorting out good from bad ideas. Also, private investors whose own money is at stake have less trouble killing bad projects than governments do.

The Right Interventions: Laying the Foundations

As discussed in chapter 5, government has been effective in supporting innovation when it has acted as a customer seeking a solution to a concrete, compelling need (e.g., that of the military). It has also been effective in supporting basic and applied research ("use-inspired" research) that has the potential for broad application. We documented many of the policies and actions the US government has pursued over the past century to lay the scientific and intellectual foundations for commercial technological development.

There are many ways the government today can help rebuild the foundations for manufacturing. One broad category includes policies that are aimed at *getting the basics right*. They include things such as dramatically improving K–12 education, reforming the tax system so that it encourages saving and investment over consumption and debt accumulation, and creating an effective plan to get government's fiscal house in order (over an appropriate period of time). These goals are absolutely necessary for the long-term economic health of the United States. We will not elaborate on these specific policies because they have been widely discussed elsewhere.[6] And, although we agree with many proposals to "get the basics right," we also think there is a lot more involved in restoring the commons.

A national economic strategy for manufacturing needs to focus on two critical foundations for the commons: scientific and technological know-how and specialized human capital. Throughout US history, the government has played critical roles in building both of these types of resources, which in turn spawned commercial economic development. When we think about sectors in which the United States has global leadership, it always comes back to the combination of superior know-how and superior human resources. How did America become a leader in the Internet? It built a massive portfolio of technological competences both by conducting decades of basic and applied research in advanced communications technology, computer architectures, electronics, and computer science and by training a veritable army of electronics engineers, computer scientists, applied mathematicians, and software engineers. The United States is a great place to do Internet-related technology and business development because it has *both* the technological capital and the human capital.

The same story has played out in the life sciences. Companies from around the world are locating their research laboratories in the United States. Why? Because of the technological know-how and human capital that resides there. Furthermore, it is there neither by accident nor some natural order of things. It is there because the US government made investments in basic and applied research (such as the Human Genome Project) and in training the world's top scientists over *decades.*

To make America the most attractive place to do complex, innovation-related manufacturing will require investments in both scientific and technological know-how and human capital. The next section discusses the role we think the government should play in doing that.

Preserving the Scientific and Technological Foundations of the Commons

The US government needs to reaffirm its long-term commitment to investing in basic and applied research. As noted in chapter 5, there are signs that this commitment is waning. However, this kind of investment is even more important than ever.

The government also needs to restore the balance of funding between basic and applied research. Historically, government funding of applied research has been just as important to US industrial competitiveness as its support of basic research. Inspired by solving difficult problems, programs such as DARPA's VLSI chip development initiative and Strategic Computing Initiative, the Department of Defense and NASA's support of the development of composites, and the NSF's funding of supercomputers are just some of the examples of applied-research projects that laid the groundwork for a broad array of commercial technological developments.

Government support of applied research is critical because these types of programs typically take long time commitments and create benefits that are not fully appropriable by any one company.

Consider the Internet, which sprang from decades-long research that was initiated by the federal government in the 1960s under the auspices of the Advanced Research Projects Agency (later renamed the Defense Advanced Research Projects Agency when it became part of the Department of Defense). ARPA was trying to build a communications network that would survive a nuclear attack. The Internet required significant investments in basic and applied research on packet switching, communications protocols, networking infrastructure, and other technologies—investments that the private sector would likely not have made because the time horizons were too long and the payoffs too unpredictable for any one company to capture.

Perhaps the decline in basic research is just a small blip, and government investment in both basic and applied research will resume its long-term trends. However, Washington's inability to deal with tax issues, entitlement reform, and discretionary spending in a constructive, nonpartisan fashion makes it hard to be optimistic. Because basic and applied research falls into the category of discretionary spending, there is a big danger that it will fall victim to budget cutters, seriously impairing the country's capacity for innovation at a time when China, Singapore, Taiwan, and some Middle Eastern countries are investing heavily to improve their scientific research infrastructure. It would be a huge mistake for the United States to assume that it can retain its leadership in science without continuing to invest.

Expanding the Commitment to Manufacturing Science and Technology

If Americans want the most advanced manufacturing to be done in the United States, then the United States must be the place where the leading-edge scientific knowledge of critical process technologies resides. Some readers may be puzzled: science and manufacturing are typically not two words that appear together in the same sentence. But process innovation can draw on advanced science as much as product innovation.

Consider the example of advanced jet engines. Today, most advanced jet engines employ esoteric materials and ceramics capable of operating under extreme heat and pressure. Manufacturing those materials is extremely complex. Much of the science underlying the processes used to make these materials was spawned by government-funded basic research in metallurgy in the 1960s.

In similar fashion, the US government needs to fund research that blazes the scientific and technological paths leading to tomorrow's innovative manufacturing. Fortunately, there is already some movement in this direction. The President's Council of Advisors on Science and Technology recently called for the federal government to create an "advanced manufacturing initiative" that would invest $500 million annually (and eventually increase the amount to $1 billion) in basic and applied research in such technologies as robotics, nanomaterials, and biomanufacturing. This is a good first step toward redressing a deficiency in our funding of manufacturing-related science. However, even at $1 billion, this is still an extremely modest investment when compared with the $143 billion that the government spends on R&D each year. And in the current budgetary climate, we are not optimistic that the council's recommendation will be accepted.

Two questions that often come up when we discuss these ideas are, How can the government know in which areas to invest? Isn't this just "targeting" under a different guise? We are not talking about investments in specific technologies (e.g., solar-photovoltaic or lithium ion battery production) by specific firms. We are talking about investments in broad technological capabilities (e.g., advanced materials, nanotechnology, biomanufacturing) that underpin a broad array of potential commercial products. Instead of trying to identify specific technical solutions, the government should try to fund many different competing scientific approaches to given technological questions.

Let's take an example: biomanufacturing, the use of biological organisms (such as genetically engineered bacteria, yeast, algae, or mammalian cells) to produce complex molecules. Many kinds of products can be produced through biomanufacturing, including pharmaceuticals, specialty chemicals, environmentally friendly fuels, and nutritional products. But biomanufacturing is still a relatively immature process technology, and the opportunities for massive productive improvements are ripe. Some biotech drugs, such as monoclonal antibodies, are extremely expensive ($300 to $5,000 per gram) to produce through current biomanufacturing methods. This is one reason why monoclonal antibody–based drugs are exorbitantly expensive (e.g., a one-year supply of Avastin, the colon-cancer drug, costs $54,000).[7]

Many US biotech companies are seeking to lower their costs by either building plants in countries that offer generous tax breaks and subsidies (e.g., Singapore and Ireland) or outsourcing production to contractors in countries such as India. But if there were major advances in basic biomanufacturing scientific know-how that drove huge breakthroughs in productivity, the temptation to move out of the United States would be much less. In fact, companies from around the world would want to locate their biomanufacturing in America so they could tap into the knowledge base.

Identifying the realms of science that may be relevant to the manufacturing of the future is by no means easy. However, there is precedent. The Human Genome Project was born from the efforts of several prominent members of the science community (including Robert Sinsheimer, LeRoy Hood, Walter Gilbert, and James Watson) who were convinced that a complete sequencing of the human genome would be a quantum leap forward for biology. However, the merits of the project were by no means a slam dunk at its outset. Some viewed sequencing the human genome as a complete waste of time, a mechanical task that involved little real science. The Human Genome Project also challenged the individual investigator-driven peer-review process used by the National Institutes of Health to allocate research funding. This was a very different way to do science, involving a large number of laboratories working in collaboration. Ultimately, after many years of debate (inside the scientific community) and the initial backing of the Department of Energy, the project was funded (and later moved to the NIH).[8]

The Human Genome Project (and similar cases, such as DARPA's Internet program) demonstrates the importance of having the scientific community deeply involved in these kinds of government funding decisions. They also demonstrate the value of stepping outside the traditional peer-review granting process for tackling big, high-risk problems that cut across traditional scientific disciplinary boundaries. Peer review certainly has its place. Unfortunately, the peer-review granting process for much of the scientific research in America is biased toward lower-risk, incremental projects ("normal science") that fit neatly into established academic fields. Currently, panels of academic scientists, each often composed of individuals from within a single discipline, make these decisions. Instead, groups comprising experts in a range of disciplines from the academic, business, and policy-making communities should be choosing the problems and deciding how best to structure research programs to seek solutions. It is especially important for government policy makers involved in these decisions to have strong scientific backgrounds.

It is widely recognized that the government has a legitimate role to play in addressing "grand challenges" that are beyond the scope of any one company or one university to solve—things such as a dependence on expensive dirty hydrocarbons, a lack of potable water, the ravages of diseases and the general need to improve health care, and the lack of dependable supplies of food in less-developed countries. Manufacturing itself faces grand challenges—for instance, manufacturing in an environmentally friendly yet economically efficient way.

These kinds of problems require long-term research and collaboration among the diverse array of organizations and companies that have pieces of expertise to contribute. Governments are often uniquely positioned to mobilize and coordinate the efforts of the numerous organizations needed to confront these huge challenges. Such government-sponsored collaborative efforts have two benefits. First, they leverage resources: a dollar spent on research goes much further when the fruits of that spending are shared broadly. Second, they help to create networks of collaborators that cut across academia and industry, which can provide a foundation for an industrial commons.

Creating the Human Capital

As noted in chapter 2, competitiveness ultimately comes down to human capital. Countries and industries do not compete; companies and people compete (and when you think about it, a "company" is really just a collection of people). The United States can only rebuild its industrial commons if it has the right kind of human capital to attract complementary investments in physical, financial, and technological capital. No one puts an R&D lab in a place where there isn't an adequate supply of first-rate scientists and engineers. No one will build a plant in a place that lacks the skilled personnel needed to operate it.

The government has a key role to play in building the human capital base needed to support the commons—one that goes beyond improving K–12 education. Let's start with the workforce in the areas of science, technology, and engineering. This group includes those with undergraduate and postgraduate degrees in science, engineering, and mathematical fields who are the foundation of any country's innovation capability in technology and manufacturing industries.

The data paints a dark picture of how well America is doing producing this kind of human capital. As of 2008 (the latest year for which data was available), the United States produced 10 percent of the world's undergraduate degrees in science and 4 percent in engineering; by comparison, the European Union's respective share was 18 percent and 17 percent, China's was 17 percent and 34 percent, and the rest of Asia was 26 percent and 17 percent.[9]

The US university system has an extraordinary capacity to train scientists and engineers. Its continuing success in attracting an enormous number of foreign students demonstrates that it also has a quality advantage. Yet many young Americans are not going into these fields. Between 1989 and 2009, 67 percent of all doctoral degrees awarded in science and engineering fields in the United States were earned by foreign residents; about half were awarded to residents from just four countries (China, India, South Korea, and Taiwan).[10] Fortunately for the US economy, the majority of these people in the past have chosen to stay in the United States.[11] In other words, the United States has become a net importer of foreign human capital. There is absolutely nothing wrong with this. An American citizen with a PhD in computer science from Stanford working in Silicon Valley has the same value to the US economy as a Chinese citizen with a PhD in computer science from Stanford working in Silicon Valley.

But this strategy of importing foreign human capital has a risk: the "stay rate" could fall. Although there is no hard evidence that the rate is now declining, two factors could change that.[12] First, as countries such as India and China continue their development in technology-intensive industries and build their scientific infrastructures, they are becoming much more attractive to their citizens who study in the United States. The second factor is US immigration policy—specifically, the availability of visas, which varies over time. The maximum cap on the number of H-1B visas, the type most frequently used by nonresident immigrants working in science and engineering fields, varies significantly from year to year (for instance, between 1995 and 2008, it varied between 65,000 per year and 195,000 per year).[13] Research by William Kerr and William Lincoln shows that increases in H–1B visas lead to higher levels of innovation in the economy.[14] US immigration policy needs to ensure that America can retain the nonresident graduates who wish to work here. It makes no sense to invest in them by providing access to world-class universities, only to send them away.

At the same time, the United States must better prepare and encourage more American students to pursue undergraduate and graduate degrees in science, technology, engineering, and mathematics (STEM). Again, better math and science training in the K–12 stage of education is essential. Beyond that, providing more funding for undergraduate scholarships and improving the quality of undergraduate teaching in these fields would help. Furthermore, to entice more STEM college graduates to stay in these fields rather than going into investment banking or management consulting, more graduate-school fellowships must be made available.

The United States also needs a government policy for training workers on the front lines of manufacturing. The kind of manufacturing at which America must excel takes much more brain than brawn, but much of the existing workforce can't do this knowledge work. When we discuss manufacturing in the United States with executives, they often tell us: "We would love to do more manufacturing in the United States, but we can't find people with the right technical skills." Tool and die makers, maintenance technicians, operators capable of working with highly sophisticated computer-controlled equipment, workers familiar with statistics, skilled welders, and even production engineers are in short supply.

The reason for such shortages is easy to understand. As manufacturing plants closed or scaled back, many people in those occupations moved on to other things or retired. Seeing fewer job opportunities down the road, young people opted for other careers. Starved of students and facing budget pressures due to cutbacks by financially strapped states, many community and vocational schools have pared their technical programs.

Government policy makers have a mind-set that manufacturing is a good sector for people with less education and training. As a result, the United States—unlike, say, Germany—spends little on training in the specialized skills required for manufacturing. This has to change.

Conclusion: Does Manufacturing Deserve Special Treatment?

Although we hope we have made our case for a national economic strategy for strengthening the foundations of manufacturing, there may still be some readers who question whether manufacturing should receive special treatment. To them we say: our proposals are about leveling the playing field rather than giving manufacturing a leg up on other sectors.

We already subsidize many service sectors of the economy and, by doing so, have tilted the field in their favor. The United States offers big subsidies for health care (e.g., employer-sponsored health care plans are paid for with pretax dollars). It has generously subsidized mortgages (e.g., by making mortgage interest tax deductible and by offering federal subsidies). The 15 percent tax rate on carried interest represents a huge subsidy to private equity. (If manufacturing profits were taxed at a maximum rate of 15 percent, manufacturing in the United States would be a lot more attractive to companies around the world.) Finally, let's not forget the massive subsidies the United States bestows on agriculture. By favoring other sectors over manufacturing, the United States is killing the manufacturing sector. There is nothing natural about this. And, as we have argued throughout this book, there is definitely nothing healthy about it.

Epilogue

We Can't Turn Back the Clock

In the classic movie *The Wizard of Oz*, there is a famous scene in which Dorothy, after landing in Oz, surveys the weird landscape and declares to her dog, "Gee Toto, I don't think we are in Kansas anymore." Someone who awoke today after thirty years of sleep might be tempted to utter something similar upon surveying the global economic landscape. There are a billion more workers in the global labor force; countries such as China, India, and Brazil—once afterthoughts in the strategies of Western companies—are now *the* critical markets to fuel growth. Once looked upon, at best, as sources of cheap labor, these countries are rapidly moving up the economic food chain. China now runs the largest trade surplus in high-technology goods. India is a global hub for software development. Brazil is coming into its own as a producer of complex mechanical goods such as aircraft and cars. And it's harder and harder to find products manufactured in America. Clearly, we don't live in Kansas anymore.

Although even the most vibrant emerging economies still face a host of their own serious challenges (e.g., massive poverty, utterly inadequate health care for the majority of the population), it is also impossible to deny that Americans today live in a far more competitive and economically challenging world than they ever have. One does not need to look far to see the strains: stagnant wages, a growing percentage of people dropping out of the workforce, ballooning deficits, and deep anxiety over the future. Pessimists see America as a country whose best days are behind it, a country that has entered a long economic sunset. There is frightening precedent: Britain was once the most innovative and vibrant economy in the world ("the workshop of the world"). On the eve of World War I, Argentina's GDP per capita ranked among the top ten in the world (and higher than that of Germany and France).[1] But after a century of economic stagnation and political turmoil, it now ranks about fiftieth.[2] Japan, once America's most feared economic rival, is well into its second "lost decade" of zero economic growth. Is America next?

The answer to that question depends on what America does. As we hope we have convinced you, there is plenty that can be done by both businesses and government to restore the American industrial commons. But everyone has a role to play. Businesses need to recognize that manufacturing is not the disposable commodity they thought; rather, it is a capability that brings competitive advantage. They should be investing in the local commons because it is in their best interests to do so. Government has to recognize the realities of the new competitive order. America cannot have a first-rate economy without first-rate intellectual and human capital.

We are often asked whether restoring American competitiveness is the job of business or government. Our answer: it is both. Americans have gotten caught in a senseless debate about the virtues of free markets versus government intervention. US history shows clearly that although the country has had one of the most market-oriented economies in the world, government policies have always played a vital complementary role in fueling economic growth.

Now is not the time to be engaging in ideological warfare over this issue. It is the time for action.

Some look to the "good old days," when Americans with relatively low skills could earn a decent living by finding a well-paying job in a factory. They look to turn back the clock by erecting barriers to trade or offering subsidies to manufacturing business to help "level the playing field." We think that would be a disaster. We can't turn back the clock. Manufacturing is not what it used to be. It is no longer a sector in which someone with a high school education can earn middle-class wages, as it was in the 1950s and 1960s. (In reality, there are fewer and fewer places in America where someone without skills and education can earn a decent living.) Manufacturing—the kind that can thrive in the United States—requires sophisticated knowledge and skills. This means that America needs to be investing in the intellectual and human capital required to do this type of manufacturing in the United States. When it comes to manufacturing, it is time to innovate, not to look backward.

The American economy has always been at its best in times of change. The globalization of the world economy is creating both unparalleled challenges and unparalleled opportunities for the American workforce. It is a much more competitive world, to be sure, but it is also a world hungering for the kind of innovation that the United States has historically been great at supplying. Throughout its history, America has demonstrated a capacity to create and reinvent sectors of the economy. Why should the industrial commons be any different?

The United States enters this more competitive world with many great strengths on its side, including a highly dynamic labor market, an entrepreneurial culture and supporting institutions (such as venture capital), the world's strongest infrastructure for scientific research, and a very large domestic market. These are enviable strengths. Economic outcomes are not a function of physical laws of nature. Decline is not inevitable; neither is prosperity. Economic outcomes are determined by the behavior, decisions, and actions of people. The future prosperity of Americans does *not* depend on what happens in China or India or any other country. American's economic fortunes in this new world order depend on what Americans choose to do.

Acknowledgments

A book such as this would not have been possible without the help and support of many people and organizations. We are deeply grateful to Steve Prokesch. Steve was the editor of our July–August 2009 *Harvard Business Review* article, "Restoring American Competitiveness," which spawned this project, and the editor of a subsequent article ("Does America Really Need Manufacturing?" *Harvard Business Review*, March 2012) that became a key piece of the book. Steve then worked closely with us during the development and writing of this book. We thank Steve for his phenomenal job editing the manuscript and for providing tough feedback along the way.

We would also like to thank Jeff Kehoe, senior editor at Harvard Business Review Press, and Adi Ignatius, editor in chief of the Harvard Business Review Group, for taking an interest in our work and giving us the chance to publish it through Harvard Business Review Press.

We are grateful to Robert Schub and Chris Allen of the Harvard Business School for their research assistance. We benefited enormously from discussions with members of the Harvard Competitive Project and want to single out Jan Rivkin for his input. We also thank Tim Solso and Ron Bloom for their comments on our work during the Harvard Competitiveness Summit and Regina Dugan for sharing her thoughts with us on the topics addressed in this book. We are grateful to Sheba Raza's assistance in the final preparation of the manuscript. We owe an intellectual debt to our former colleagues Kim Clark, Robert Hayes, and Steven Wheelwright, who were pioneers in this field and whose work deeply influenced us. As always, we are grateful to the Harvard Business School Division of Research for generously funding and supporting our research. We owe Dean Nitin Nohria a special note of thanks for his support not only of our work, but also of the Harvard Business School's research on the topic of competitiveness.

Finally, we would like to thank our wives—Alice Rosa and Julie Shih—for their support throughout this project. We started this endeavor three years ago as an article. We promised them then that things would return to normal as soon as we got that piece finished. Then we decided to write this book. Throughout this marathon, we promised Alice and Julie (repeatedly) that the proverbial light at the end of the tunnel was visible and that things would soon return to normal. We suspect that all along they knew the tunnel was a bit longer, but their encouragement and patience were unwavering. It is to both of them that we dedicate this book.

Appendix: Key Component Suppliers for Photovoltaic Unit (India)

Main components in photovoltaic module	Brand	Country of manufacture
Solar cells	Make own, multiple sources	India, China
EVA (ethylene vinyl acetate)	Etimex Solar GmbH (now Solutia Solar GmbH), owned by Solutia, St. Louis, MO	Germany
	Mitsui Chemical Fabro, Nagoya Works	Japan
	Sekisui Chemical Co., Ltd.	Japan
	Bixcure from Tomark Industries; Bixby International Corporation, Newburyport, MA	USA

	Yang Yi Science & Technology Co., Ltd.	Taipei, Taiwan
	STR Solar	USA (Enfield, CT)
Back sheet	Isovolta	Austria
	Toyo aluminum	Japan/China
	Keiwa Inc.	Japan
	Krempel GmbH	Germany
	Madico Specialty Films, subsidiary of Lintec of Japan	USA (Woburn, MA)
	Taiflex Scientific Co. Ltd.	Taiwan
	Toppan Printing	Japan
	Reiko	Japan
Glass	Saint Gobain	India
	CSG (China Southern Glass) Holding Co., CSG PVTech Co., Ltd.	China
	Ashai Glass Co., Ltd.	Japan
	NSG	Japan
	Stanley Glass Co., Ltd.	Taiwan
Aluminum frame	SEECO	
	Xijie	China
	Other makers	China

Ribbon, solar cell tabbing, and string interconnect ribbons	Ulbrich Precision Flat Wire	USA
	Creativ	Argentina
Junction-box/cable	Tyco	Germany
	Coyo Corp.	Taiwan
	Yukita Electric Wire Co., Ltd.	Japan/China
	Yamaichi	Japan/Germany
	Onamba Co. Ltd.	Japan/Vietnam
	Huber+Suhner AG	Switzerland/China
	Bizlink Taiwan International Corp.	China/Taiwan

Source: Data courtesy of Moser Baer Solar Limited.

Notes

Prologue

1. Data from the Bureau of Economic Analysis.

2. The term "post-industrial society" was coined by Harvard sociologist Daniel Bell in his book *The Coming of Post-Industrial Society: A Venture in Social Forecasting* (New York: Basic Books, 1973).

3. Calculated with data from National Science Foundation, "New Employment Statistics for the 2008 Business R&D and Innovation Survey," NSF 10-326, July 2010, and data on the total workforce in 2010.

Chapter 1

1. Gary P. Pisano and Willy C. Shih, "Restoring American Competitiveness," *Harvard Business Review*, July–August 2009, 114–125.

2. See, for example, M. L. Dertouzos, R. K. Lester, and R. M. Solow, *Made in America* (Cambridge, MA: MIT Press, 1989); R. Z. Lawrence, *Can America Compete?* (Washington, DC: Brookings Institution, 1984); B. R. Scott, "National Strategy for Stronger US Competitiveness," *Harvard Business Review*, March–April 1984, 77–91; J. A. Young, "Technology and Competitiveness: A Key to the Economic Future of the United States," *Science* 241, no. 4863 (1988): 313–316; and J. A. Young, "Global Competition: The New Reality," *California Management Review* 27, no. 3 (1985): 11–25.

3. World Trade Organization, *International Trade Statistics 2009* (Geneva: World Trade Organization, 2009), 62, 121, http://www.wto.org/english/res_e/statis_e/its2009_e/its09_toc_e.htm.

4. National Science Board, *Science and Engineering Indicators 2012* (Arlington, VA: National Science Foundation, 2012), http://www.nsf.gov/statistics/seind12/.

5. See, for example, Clyde Prestowitz, *The Betrayal of American Prosperity: Free Market Delusions, America's Decline, and How We Must Compete in the Post-Dollar Era* (New York: Free Press, 2010).

6. 1992 was the first year such data became available on a consistent basis for China; 2009 was the last full year this data was available at the time of this writing. The World Bank uses a similar definition for "high-technology" sectors as used in the earlier analyses in this chapter.

7. J. Perlin, *The Silicon Solar Cell Turns 50*, National Renewable Energy Lab, NREL report no. BR-520-33947, August 2004, http://www. nrel.gov/docs/fy04osti/33947.pdf.

8. US Department of Energy, *2008 Solar Technologies Market Report* (Washington, DC: US Department of Energy, January 2010).

9. US Census Bureau trade data.

10. Keith Bradsher, "Solar Panel Maker Moves Work to China," *New York Times*, January 14, 2011; Russell Gold, "Overrun by Chinese Rivals, US Solar Company Falters," *Wall Street Journal*, August 17, 2011; and Peg Brickley, "Evergreen Solar to Abandon Massachusetts Factory," *Wall Street Journal*, March 12, 2012.

11. J. Bhagwati, "The Manufacturing Fallacy," Project Syndicate, August 27, 2010, http://www.project-syndicate.org/commentary/the-manufacturing-fallacy.

12. G. Hardin, "The Tragedy of the Commons," *Science* 162 (1968): 1243–1247; D. Feeny, F. Berkes, B. McCay, and J. Acheson, "The Tragedy of the Commons—22 Years Later," *Human Ecology* 18, no. 1 (1990): 1–19; E. Ostrom, "Coping with Tragedies of the Commons," *Annual Review of Political Science* 2 (1999): 493–535; and E. Ostrom, J. Burger, C. Field, R. Norgaard, and D. Policansky, "Sustainability—Revisiting the Commons: Local Lessons, Global Challenges," *Science* 284, no. 5412 (1999): 278–282.

13. Thomas L. Friedman. *The World Is Flat: A Brief History of the Twenty-First Century* (New York: Farrar, Straus and Giroux, 2006).

14. K. Bourzac, "Applied Materials Moves Solar Expertise to China," *Technology Review*, December 22, 2009.

15. Ralph J. Brodd, *Factors Affecting U.S. Production Decisions: Why Are There No Volume Lithium-Ion Battery Manufacturers in the United States?* NIST GCR 06-903 (Gaithersburg, MD: National Institutes of Standards and Technology, December 2006), http://www.atp.nist.gov/eao/gcr06-903.pdf.

16. See, for example, Vannevar Bush, *Science: The Endless Frontier* (Washington, DC: Government Printing Office, 1945); Thomas Arrison, *Rising Above the Gathering Storm Two Years Later: Accelerating Progress Toward a Brighter Economic Future* (Washington, DC: National Academies Press, 2009); and Daniel Kevles, "The National Science Foundation and the Debate over Postwar Research Policy, 1942–1945, A Political Interpretation of *Science: The Endless Frontier*," *Isis* 68, no. 1 (1977): 4–26.

17. G. Garrett, "Globalization's Missing Middle," *Foreign Affairs* 83, no. 6 (2004): 84–96; and J. VandeHei, "Kerry Donors Include 'Benedict Arnolds': Candidate Decries Tax-Haven Firms While Accepting Executives' Aid," *Washington Post*, February 26, 2004.

Chapter 2

1. Michael Porter, *The Competitive Advantage of Nations* (New York: Free Press, 1998); Paul Krugman, "Competitiveness: A Dangerous Obsession," *Foreign Affairs* 73, no. 2 (1994): 28–44.

2. Laura D. Tyson, *Who's Bashing Whom? Trade Conflict in High Technology Industries* (Washington, DC: Institute for International Economics, 1992).

3. Krugman, "Competitiveness."

4. Kevin B. Barefoot and Marilyn Ibarra-Caton, "Direct Investment Positions for 2010: Country and Industry Detail," *Survey of Current Business* 91, no. 7 (2011): 125–141.

5. Analyzed from data downloaded from the US Bureau of the Census, Geographic Mobility 2008 to 2009, http://www.census.gov/population/www/socdemo/migrate/cps2009.html.

6. European Commission, *Geographic Mobility in the European Union: Optimising Its Economic and Social Benefits*, Contract VT/2006/04 (Brussels: European Commission, April 2008).

7. Michael E. Porter, *Competitive Strategy: Techniques for Analyzing Industries and Competitors* (New York: Free Press, 1980).

8. Central Intelligence Agency, *World Economic Factbook 2010*, https://www.cia.gov/library/publications/download/download-2010/index.html.

9. Ibid.

10. "Labor Force Statistics from the Current Population Survey," Bureau of Labor Statistics, http://data.bls.gov/pdq/SurveyOutputServlet.

11. Ibid.; and data on trading partners from Central Intelligence Agency, *World Factbook*, https://www.cia.gov/library/publications/the-world-factbook.

12. Krugman, "Competitiveness."

13. Michael Spence and Sandile Hlatshwayo, "The Evolving Structure of the US Economy and the Employment Challenge," working paper, Council on Foreign Relations, New York, March 2011.

14. Ibid., 4.

15. National Science Board, *Science and Engineering Indicators 2010* (Arlington, VA: National Science Foundation, 2010); and Robert Barro and Jong-Wha Lee, "International Data on Educational Attainment: Updates and Implications," working paper 7911, National Bureau of Economic Research, Cambridge, MA, September 2000.

16. National Science Board, "Research and Development: National Trends and International Linkages," in *Science Indicators 2010* (Arlington,VA: National Science Foundation, 2010), http://www.nsf.gov/statistics/seind10/c4/c4s5.htm.

17. Ibid.

18. Kevin B. Barefoot and Raymond J. Mataloni Jr., "Operations of U.S. Multinational Companies in the United States and Abroad: Preliminary Results from the 2009 Benchmark Survey," *Survey of Current Business*, November 2011, 29–48, http://www.bea.gov/scb/pdf/2011/11%20November/1111_mnc.pdf.

19. Ross Perot, *Save Your Job, Save Our Country: Why NAFTA Must Be Stopped—Now* (New York: Hyperion Books, 1993).

20. John Harwood, "53% in US Say Free Trade Hurts Nation: NBC/WSJ Poll," CNBC, September 28, 2010, http://www.cnbc.com/id/39407846/53_in_US_Say_Free_Trade_Hurts_Nation_NBC_WSJ_Poll.

21. European Commission, "South Korea," http://ec.europa.eu/trade/creating-opportunities/bilateral-relations/countries/korea/.

22. Clyde Prestowitz, *The Betrayal of American Prosperity* (New York: Free Press, 2010). The Republic of Korea-United States Free Trade Agreement was eventually approved by the US Senate in October 2011 (http://www.ustr.gov/trade-agreements/free-trade-agreements/korus-fta).

23. Dale W. Jorgenson, Mun S. Ho, and Kevin J. Stiroh, "A Retrospective Look at the US Productivity Growth Resurgence," *Journal of Economic Perspectives* 22, no. 1 (2008): 3–24.

24. The "potato chips versus semiconductor chips" debate is attributed to a remark made by Michael Boskin, President George H. W. Bush's Chair of the Council of Economic Advisors, who is alleged to have said that it did not matter whether the United States made semiconductors chips or potato chips.

25. Daniel Bell, *The Coming of Post-Industrial Society: A Venture in Social Forecasting* (New York: Basic Books, 1973).

26. James Cook, "You Mean We've Been Speaking Prose All These Years?" *Forbes*, April 11, 1983, 146, quoted in Stephen S. Cohen and John Zysman, *Manufacturing Matters: The Myth of the Post-Industrial Economy* (New York: Basic Books, 1987), 5.

27. Other prominent economists who share this view include Jagdish Bhagwati of Columbia University (see, for example, his blog post "The Manufacturing Fallacy," August 27, 2010, http://www.project-syndicate.org/commentary/bhagwati3/English) and Christine Romer (see, for example, her op-ed "Do Manufacturers Need Special Treatment?" *New York*

Times, February 4, 2012, http://www.nytimes.com/2012/02/05/business/do-manufacturers-need-special-treatment-economic-view.html).

28. Richard McCormack, "Council on Competitiveness Says U.S. Has Little to Fear but Fear Itself; By Most Measures, U.S. Is Way Ahead of Global Competitors," *Manufacturing & Technology News*, November 30, 2006, http://www.manufacturingnews.com/news/06/1130/art1.html.

Chapter 3

1. Elinor Ostrom, Christopher B. Field, Richard B. Norgaard, and David Policansky, "Revisiting the Commons: Local Lessons, Global Challenges," *Science* 284, no. 5412 (1999): 278–282.

2. David A. Hounshell, *From the American System to Mass Production, 1800–1932* (Baltimore, MD: The Johns Hopkins University Press, 1984).

3. John S. Heckman, "The Product Cycle and New England Textiles," *Quarterly Journal of Economics* 94, no. 4 (1980): 697–717.

4. George S. Gibb, *The Saco-Lowell Shops* (Cambridge, MA: Harvard University Press, 1950).

5. Pratt & Whitney Company, *Accuracy for Seventy Years: 1860–1930* (Hartford, CT: Pratt & Whitney Company, 1930).

6. Germany Trade & Invest, *The Automotive Industry in Germany: Industry Overview 2010* (Berlin: Germany Trade & Invest, 2010).

7. See Nathan Rosenberg, "Technological Change in the Machine Tool Industry, 1840–1910," *Journal of Economic History* 23, no. 4 (1963): 414–443.

8. See, for example, Timothy Bresnahan and Manuel Trajtenberg, "General Purpose Technologies 'Engines of Economic Growth'?" *Journal of Econometrics* 65, no. 1 (1995): 83–108.

9. David Mowery and Nathan Rosenberg, *Paths of Innovation: Technological Change in 20th Century America* (New York: Cambridge University Press, 1998).

10. Alfred Marshall, *Principles of Economics* (London: MacMillan, 1890).

11. Paul Krugman, "Increasing Returns and Economic Geography," *Journal of Political Economy* 99, no. 3 (1991): 483–499.

12. Thomas L. Friedman, *The World Is Flat: A Brief History of the Twenty-First Century* (New York: Farrar, Straus and Giroux, 2005).

13. Pankaj Ghemawat, *World 3.0: Global Prosperity and How to Achieve It* (Boston: Harvard Business Review Press, 2011).

14. Michael E. Porter, *On Competition* (Boston: Harvard Business School Publishing, 1999).

15. Michael Polanyi, *Personal Knowledge: Towards a Post-Critical Philosophy* (Chicago: University of Chicago Press, 1958).

16. Richard Nelson and Sidney Winter, *An Evolutionary Theory of Economic Change* (Cambridge, MA: Harvard University Press, 1982).

17. On the Toyota production system, see Steven Spear and Kent H. Bowen, "Decoding the DNA of the Toyota Production System," *Harvard Business Review*, September–October 1999, 96–106.

18. D. B. Audretsch, "Agglomeration and the Location of Innovative Activity," *Oxford Review of Economic Policy* 14, no. 2 (1998): 18–29.

19. Stefano Breschi and Francesco Lissoni, "Mobility of Skilled Workers and Co-Invention Networks: An Anatomy of Localized Knowledge Flows," *Journal of Economic Geography* 9, no. 4 (2009): 439–468.

20. On the use of the ecosystem metaphor to analyze economic systems and industries, see (among many) Michael Hannan and John Freeman, "The Population Ecology of Organizations," *American Journal of Sociology* 82, no. 5 (1977): 929–964; Marco Iansiti and Roy Levien, *The Keystone Advantage: What the New Dynamics of Business Ecosystems Mean for Strategy, Innovation, and Sustainability* (Boston: Harvard Business School Press, 2004); and Rosabeth Moss Kanter, "Enriching the Ecosystem," *Harvard Business Review*, March–April 2012.

Chapter 4

1. On the concept of modularity in design, see Carliss Baldwin and Kim Clark, *Design Rules, Volume 1: The Power of Modularity* (Cambridge, MA: MIT Press, 2000).

2. The discussion in this chapter draws heavily from the authors' article "Does America Really Need Manufacturing?" *Harvard Business Review*, March–April 2012.

3. Gary P. Pisano, *The Development Factory: Unlocking the Potential of Process Innovation* (Boston: Harvard Business School Press, 1996).

4. Maureen McKelvey, *Evolutionary Innovations: The Business of Biotechnology* (New York: Oxford University Press, 2000).

5. R. Courtland, "ICs Grow Up," *Spectrum, IEEE* 49, no. 1 (2012): 33–35.

Chapter 5

1. David A. Hounshell, *From the American System to Mass Production, 1800–1932* (Baltimore, MD: The Johns Hopkins University Press, 1984).

2. William Lazonick, "Nine Government Investments That Made Us an Industrial Leader," *Next New Deal*, September 8, 2011, http://www.

newdeal20.org/2011/09/08/nine-government-investments-that-made-us-an-industrial-economic-leader-57814/.

3. Alfred Chandler, *Scale and Scope: The Dynamics of Industrial Capitalism* (Cambridge, MA: Harvard University Press, 1990).

4. Ibid.

5. Alfred Chandler, *The Visible Hand: The Managerial Revolution in American Business* (Cambridge, MA: Belknap Press of Harvard University Press, 1977).

6. Chandler, *Scale and Scope*. As Chandler points out, capitalism took different forms in Europe during the same period. Britain, for instance, continued to rely on personal capitalism in which enterprises continued to be owned and managed by the same person or family. In practice, this meant that British corporations could not access capital on the same scale as their American counterparts.

7. Ibid.

8. Ibid.

9. David Mowery and Nathan Rosenberg, *Paths of Innovation: Technological Change in 20th Century America* (New York: Cambridge University Press, 1998).

10. Hounshell, *From the American System to Mass Production*.

11. Mowery and Rosenberg, *Paths of Innovation*.

12. David Mowery, "The Relationship Between Contractual and Intrafirm Forms of Industrial Research in American Manufacturing, 1921–1946," *Explorations in Economic History* 20 (1983): 351–374.

13. Richard R. Nelson and Gavin Wright, "The Rise and Fall of American Technological Leadership: The Postwar Era in Historical Perspective," *Journal of Economic Literature* 30, no. 4 (1992): 1931–1964.

14. David Hounshell reminds us that this view overlooked the enormous engineering and manufacturing know-how and capabilities of the nation's corporations, without which none of these new technologies and products could have emerged.

15. Daniel J. Kevles, "The National Science Foundation and the Debate over Postwar Research Policy, 1942–1945: A Political Interpretation of *Science: The Endless Frontier*," *Isis* 68, no. 1 (1977): 4–26.

16. Nelson and Wright, "Rise and Fall."

17. Franco Malerba, *The Semiconductor Business: The Economics of Rapid Growth and Decline* (London: MacMillan, 1985).

18. Jeffrey Macher, David Mowery, and Alberto Di Minin, "The Non-Globalization of Innovation, I: The Semiconductor Industry," *California Management Review* 50, no. 1 (2007): 217–242.

19. C. F. Yinug, "The Rise of the Flash Memory Market: Its Impact on Firm Behavior and Global Semiconductor Trade Patterns," *Journal of International Commerce & Economics* 1 (2008): 137–162.

20. Today only Micron Technology still makes DRAMs in the United States.

21. Willy C. Shih, Gary P. Pisano, and Andrew A. King, "Radical Collaboration: IBM Microelectronics Joint Development Alliances," Case 608–121 (Boston: Harvard Business School, 2008).

22. Jim O'Neill and Anna Stupnytska, "The Long-Term Outlook for the BRICs and N-11 Post Crisis," Goldman Sachs Global Economics Paper 192, December 4, 2009, 22.

23. Ibid., 6.

24. See the website of the Ministry of Science and Technology of the People's Republic of China, http://www.most.gov.cn/eng/programmes1/200610/t20061009_36225.htm.

25. See Willy Shih's testimony in *2009 Report to Congress of the U.S.-China Economic and Security Review Commission*, 111th Congress, 1st session, November 2009, 87–88.

26. National Science Board, "Key Science and Engineering Indicators—2010 Digest," National Science Foundation Publication NSB 10-02 (Arlington, VA: National Science Foundation, 2010).

27. Scott J. Weisbenner, "Corporate Share Repurchases in the 1990s: What Role Do Stock Options Play?" working paper, Federal Reserve Board, Washington, DC, 2000.

28. Kevin B. Barefoot and Raymond J. Mataloni Jr., "Operations of US Multinational Companies in the United States and Abroad: Preliminary Results for the 2009 Benchmark Survey," *Survey of Current Business*, November 2011, 29–48, http://www.bea.gov/scb/pdf/2011/11%20November/1111_mnc.pdf.

29. Michael Spence and Sandile Hlatshwayo, "The Evolving Structure of the US Economy and the Employment Challenge," working paper, Council on Foreign Relations, New York, March 2011, 33.

Chapter 6

1. On this theme of capabilities in competition, see Robert Hayes, Steven Wheelwright, and Kim Clark, *Dynamic Manufacturing* (New York: Free Press, 1990); C. K. Prahalad and Gary Hamel, "Core Competences of the Corporation," *Harvard Business Review*, May–June 1990, 79–91; and David Teece, Gary Pisano, and Amy Shuen, "Dynamic Capabilities and Strategic Management," *Strategic Management Journal* 18, no. 7 (1997): 509–533.

2. On the role of commitment in strategy, see Pakaj Ghemawat, *Commitment: The Dynamics of Strategy* (New York: Free Press, 1991).

3. Michael E. Porter and Jan W. Rivkin, "The Looming Challenge to U.S. Competitiveness," *Harvard Business Review*, March 2012, 87.

4. This section draws heavily from our article "Does America Really Need Manufacturing?" *Harvard Business Review*, March–April 2012.

5. Gary P. Pisano, *Science Business: The Promise, the Reality, and the Future of Biotech* (Boston: Harvard Business School Press, 2006).

6. Mihir Desai, "The Incentive Bubble," *Harvard Business Review*, March 2012.

Chapter 7

1. On the need for a national economic strategy, see Michael Porter, "Why America Needs an Economic Strategy," *Bloomberg Businessweek*, October 30, 2012.

2. Michael E. Porter, "What Is Strategy?" *Harvard Business Review*, November 1996, 61–78.

3. David C. Mowery and Richard R. Nelson, eds., *The Sources of Industrial Leadership: Studies of Seven Industries* (Cambridge: Cambridge University Press, 1999).

4. Franco Malerba, *The Semiconductor Business* (Madison: University of Wisconsin Press, 1985).

5. The European initiative led to the production of the Concorde aircraft, which was only sold to British Airways and Air France (with heavy purchase subsidies).

6. See, for example, the March 2012 issue of *Harvard Business Review*.

7. Chris Chen, "Challenges and Opportunities of Monoclonal Antibody Production in China," *Trends in Bio/Pharmaceutical Industry* 5, no. 3 (2009): 28–33, http://tbiweb.org/tbi/file_dir/TBI2009/Challenge%20in%20China.pdf.

8. Leslie Roberts, "Controversial from the Start," *Science* 291, no. 5507 (2001): 1182–1188.

9. National Science Board, *Science and Engineering Indicators 2012* (Arlington, VA: National Science Foundation, 2012), 1–7.

10. Ibid., 2–29.

11. Michael Finn, "Stay Rates of Foreign Doctoral Recipients from US Universities, 2007," working paper, Oak Ridge Institute for Science and Technology, Oak Ridge, TN, January 2010.

12. Ibid.

13. W. Kerr and W. Lincoln, "The Supply Side of Innovation: H–1B Visa Reforms and US Ethnic Innovation," *Journal of Labor Economics* 28, no. 3 (2010): 473–508.

14. Ibid.

Epilogue

1. "Argentina's Collapse: A Decline Without Parallel," *The Economist*, February 28, 2002, http://www.economist.com/node/1010911.

2. International Monetary Fund, World Economic Outlook Database, September 2011, http://www.imf.org/external/pubs/ft/weo/2011/02/weodata/index.aspx.

Index

advanced manufacturing
initiative, 127
aerospace industry, 2, 51
"agglomerating forces," 53–55
Alenia Aeronautica, 114
American Revolution, 46
American system of manufactures,
46, 73–75
Amgen, 68–69
antitrust laws, 76–77
Apple, 70, 106
Applied Materials, 15, 83
arbitrage, 97–98
Arco, 8
Arkwright, Richard, 54
Armani, 115
armories, federal, 46, 73–74
assets
hard, flight from, 96–97
shared complementary, 58–59
AT&T, 76, 77
automobiles
electric, 16, 48
Toyota production system for,
57, 107

bailouts, 88, 120
balance of trade, 3–5, 135
batteries, rechargeable, 10, 11–12,
16, 51
Bell, Daniel, 42

Bell Labs, 8
Biogen Idec, 24
biomanufacturing, 128–129
"bio-similars," 115
biotechnology, 2, 55, 68–69,
115, 116
boards of directors, 117
Boeing, 8, 114, 116
Brazil, 29–30, 85, 86, 135
Breschi, Stefano, 57
building versus buying, 97–99, 104
Bureau of Economic Analysis, 35,
94–95
Bush, Vannevar, 78
buy versus build decisions,
97–99, 104

Canon, 82
capabilities
buying, 107
competing through, 103–107
consumer electronics and, 49–50
erosion of, vicious circle in, 16
industry linkages and flow of,
47–49
for innovation, 14–15
innovation connected with, 12
loss of in United States, 9–13
management in building,
104–107
proximity and, 52–57

capabilities (*continued*)
  shared, xiv
  skilled workforce, 33–36
  strategic value of, 108–109
  value of, 104
capital
  deepening, labor productivity
    and, 40–41
  investments, 90–95
  mobility of, 26
Census Bureau. *See* US Census
  Bureau
challenges, grand, 129–130
Chandler, Alfred, 74–75, 101
chemical vapor deposition
  (CVD), 49
China, 85
  balance of trade with, 19
  educated workforce in, 34–36
  electronics manufacturing in, 83
  growing middle class in, 37
  labor supply in, 29–30
  market growth in, 86, 135
  National Plan on Key Basic Re-
    search and Development, 87
  National Program on Key Basic
    Research Project, 87
  State High-Tech Development
    Plan, 87–88
  trade policies of, 6–8, 19, 120
Chinon Industries, 71
Chrysler, 88, 120
clustering, geographic, 53–56
Cohen, Stephen, ix
collaboration, 130
commitment, 98, 106–107, 126–130
commons, 13, 45. *See also*
  industrial commons
communication
  face-to-face, 57
  systems for, 74

comparative advantage trade
  theory, 24
compensation, executive, 116
competitiveness, xiii, 21–44
  analysis of, 28–29
  capabilities in, 103–107
  concerns over, 21
  countries' advantages in, 25–26
  of countries and companies,
    22–24
  definition of, 21
  globalization and, 28–44
  human capital in, 25–28
  implications of and reactions to,
    36–44
  loss of US, 1–2, 3–8
  services in, 42–44
  tests of, 25
  trying to turn back the clock on,
    36–38
components, process innovation
  and, 70–72, 141–143
consumer electronics, 16
  capabilities underlying, 49–50
  manufacturing technology
    rejuvenation in, 113–114
  semiconductor industry and,
    82–84
Corning, 97
corporations, formation of,
  74–75, 77
cost structures, 106–107
cultural barriers, 27
currency devaluations, 25
customers, strategic value of, 108

decision making, xii
  capabilities-based, 104
  national loyalty in, 20
deep relationships, 104

Defense Advanced Research
    Projects Agency (DARPA),
    82–83, 125
de-industrialization, 2–3
Dell, 106
demand pull linkages, 49, 51
demodularization, 114
Department of Defense. *See* US
    Department of Defense
Department of Energy. *See* US
    Department of Energy
Desai, Mihir, 116
devaluations, 25
digital photography, 70–72
digitization, 5
distribution, 77
dividend/stock buybacks, 91–95
DuPont, 65, 76, 77
dynamic random-access memory
    chips (DRAMs), 80–81, 82

economic geography, 53–54
economic growth, 15–16, 135–137
economic performance, xiii, 31,
    51–52
ecosystems, 58–60
education, 33–36, 75–76, 79, 108
    government policy in, 124,
        130–133
    international comparisons in,
        86–88
Endless Frontier, The (Bush), 78
energy sector, 8–13, 122–123
engineering, 2, 131
entrepreneurs, 2, 137–138
Evergreen Solar, 9–10, 123
exogenous circumstances, 60, 73

factor input markets, 22–23
factor mobility, 26–28
fashion apparel industry, 115

Ferragamo, 115
fiber optics, 12
financial services, 55–56
"fin" field effect transistors
    (FinFETs), 69
First Solar, 9
flat world concept, 13–14, 54–55
Ford Motor Company, 58, 59
foreign direct investment (FDI), 35
forgings, ultra-heavy, 11
Freescale Semiconductor, 83
free trade, 18, 19
    government policy and, 19–20
    trying to turn back the clock on,
        36–38
Friedman, Thomas, 54–55
funding, 73
    government in, 77–80, 89–90,
        123–130
    scientific community in, 129

gallium arsenide (GaAs) laser
    diodes, 12
General Electric, 76, 77, 115
General Motors, 58, 59, 88, 120
general-purpose technologies,
    51–52
Genzyme, 24
Ghemawat, Pankaj, 55
GI Bill, 79
Gilbert, Walter, 128
glass, precision, 12
globalization, 18
    competitiveness increased by,
        28–44
    economic change from, 84–88
    local commons in, 102–103,
        108–109
    services and, 42–44
    trying to turn back the clock on,
        36–38

government policy, xii, xiv–xv,
119–133
American system of manufactures
and, 46
antitrust, 76–77
Chinese, 6–8
economic growth and, 136–137
foundations for, 123–125
free markets and, 19–20
Great Recession and, 1
in human capital building,
124–125, 130–133
on immigration, 131–132
international comparisons of,
86–90
laissez-faire versus centralized,
119–120
patent, 76–77
on research funding, 73, 89–90,
123–126
in rise and decline of industrial
commons, 17–18, 73
targeting in, 122–123, 127–128
taxes and subsidies, 81–82
on trade, 6–8, 19
wrong interventions in, 122–123
"grand challenges," 129–130
Great Recession of 2008, x, 1, 41–42
gross domestic product (GDP)
manufacturing as percentage of, ix
services as percentage of, 43
trade as percentage of, 30–31
trade deficit and, 3–4

H-1B visas, 131–132
hard assets, 96–97
hard skills, 96, 97
Hayes, Robert, ix
Hewlett-Packard, 106
high tech, in balance of trade, 7
Hlatshwayo, Sandile, 32–33, 43, 97

Hood, LeRoy, 128
human capital, xv
in competitiveness, 25–28
economic rewards of
competitiveness to, 23
foreign, importing, 131–132
government policy and,
124–125, 130–133
mobility of, 27–28
Human Genome Project, 128–129

IBM, 8, 82
immigration policy, 131–132
India, 85
educated workforce in, 34–36
growing middle class in, 37
labor supply in, 29–30
market growth in, 86, 135
photovoltaics in, 141–143
industrial commons, xii, 45–60
attracted by, 14
businesses in erosion of, 90–95
capabilities in, xiv
commitment to, 98, 106–107
definition of, 2, 45
delicate equilibrium of, 58–60
erosion of, 2–3, 12–18
forces in rise and decline of, 73
geographic proximity and, 52–57
global economy and, 84–88
growth of early American, 46
as growth platform, 15–16
industry linkages in, 47–52
for innovation, 12
local, 13–14, 44
in location decisions, 46
management in rebuilding,
101–118
private versus social returns in,
58–60
rejuvenating, xiv

rise and decline of, xiv, 73–99
scientific and technological
    foundations of, 125–126
in semiconductors, 14, 49, 52,
    80–84
strategic value of, 108–109
industrial districts, 53–55
industrial revolution, 51
industry linkages, xiii–xiv
information flows, 47, 52–57
information technology (IT), 3
    balance of trade in, 19
    labor markets for outsourcing, 35
    productivity growth in, 40
infrastructure, 2, 137–138
    geographic proximity and, 53
    for photovoltaic cells, 9–10
innovation
    capabilities for, 14–15
    geographic proximity and, 53–57
    government in, 123–125
    industrial commons in, 14
    industry linkages and, 48
    manufacturing's connections to,
        xi–xii
    process, 62–71
    process-driven, 66, 68–70
    process-embedded, 66–68, 70, 71
    pure process, 67
    pure product, 66–67
    US dominance in, 2, 61
    when manufacturing is critical
        to, 60, 61–72
input–output analysis, 47
integrated design manufacturers
    (IDMs), 83
Intel, 69, 81, 83–84, 96
intellectual property, 47, 76–77
interchangeable parts, 46, 73–74
intercontinental ballistic missiles
    (ICBMs), 79

Internet, ix, 3, 56, 124
iPad, 70

Japan, ix
    camera industry in, 70–72
    competitiveness of, 3
    economic growth in, 136
    high tech in, 7
    Ministry of International Trade
        and Industry, 82, 123
    semiconductors in, 82
jet engines, 127
jobs
    manufacturing's impact on, x–xi
    preservation of, 121
    in services, 43–44
Johnson & Johnson, 113
Jorgenson, Dale, 39, 41, 42

Kerr, William, 132
Kerry, John, 20
Kevlar, 65
KLA-Tencor, 83
knowledge. See also education
    government policy and, 124–125
    industry linkages and flow of, 47
    proximity and movement of,
        52–57
    tacit, 56–57
    transfer of, 56–57
knowledge work/workers, xi
    competitiveness via services and,
        42–44
    manufacturing versus, 2–3
    natural progression toward,
        10, 13
Kodak, 70–72
Krugman, Paul, 25, 31, 53–54
Kulicke & Soffa Industries, 83
Kyocera, 9–10

labor markets, 22–23, 137–138
　capital deepening and, 40–41
　education and, 33–36
　expansion of trade and, 30–33
　geographic proximity and
　　pooling of, 53
　global competition in, 29–44
　local, 30
　trying to turn back the clock on,
　　36–38
　US workers in, 32–33
labor productivity, 38
laissez-faire, 119–120
Land Grant College Act (1862),
　75–76
language barriers, 27
leadership, 115–118
Leontief, Wassily, 47
life sciences, 55, 124–125
light emitting diodes (LEDs), 12, 49
Lincoln, William, 132
linkages, industry, 47–52
liquid crystal displays (LCDs), 12
Lissoni, Francesco, 57
living standards, 23, 25, 37
location decisions, 14
　industrial commons in, 46
　proximity of R&D in, 103
　for R&D, 15
　real costs in, 107–115
　trend assessment in, 112–115
long-term versus short-term
　interests, 103, 115–118

machine tools, 10, 11, 48
management
　in competitiveness, 20
　in erosion of industrial
　　commons, 17–18, 95–99
　leadership and, 115–118
　for long-term interests, 115–118

professional, rise of, 101
　in rebuilding the commons,
　　101–118
　in rise and decline of industrial
　　commons, 73, 77
manufacturing
　American system of, 46, 73–75
　as cost center, 107–108
　debates over importance of, x–xii
　government policy on, 119–133
　interdependence of R&D with,
　　62–69
　job impact of, x–xi
　location decisions, 14–15, 46,
　　103, 107–115
　as low-value-added work, 44
　maturity of processes and, 63,
　　65–69
　modularity of, 63–65, 109–111
　natural decline in, 10, 13
　outsourcing, 5–8
　as percentage of GDP, ix
　services versus, 42–44
　technology rejuvenation in,
　　113–114
　trade deficit and, 4–8
　US investments in, 94–95
　when it's critical to innovation,
　　60, 61–72
Manufacturing Matters (Zysman and
　Cohen), ix
markets
　analysis of, management based
　　on, 103
　changing size of, 85–86
　national, 74, 137–138
Marshall, Alfred, 53, 55
Massachusetts Institute of
　Technology (MIT), 76
mass production, 46, 73–74, 77
Matsushita, 71

maturity, of processes, 63, 65–69,
    109–111, 114–115
MaxMara, 115
medical technology, 2
metal-organic chemical vapor
    deposition (MOCVD), 49
Micron Technology, 81, 82
migration, internal, 29
mobility, factor, 26–28
modularity–maturity matrix, 66,
    109–111, 114–115
monoclonal antibodies, 128
Morrill Act (1862), 75–76
motors and generators, 11
multinationals, 102
    buying versus building by, 97–98

NASA, 125
national champions, 122
National Institutes of Health
    (NIH), 18, 77, 129
nationalism, 20, 102
National Renewable Energy
    Laboratory (NREL), 8, 9
National Science Foundation, 6,
    18, 34, 77, 90, 125
Nikon, 82
Nippon Telegraph and Telephone
    (NTT), 82
Nittō Kōgaku, 71
nontradable sectors, 32–33
North American Free Trade
    Agreement (NAFTA), 36
Novartis, 109
NVIDIA, 83

Obama, Barack, 120, 121
on-the-job training, 132–133
operations, board knowledge
    about, 117
orderly market agreements, 88

organizations, mobility of, 27
outsourcing
    modularity and, 115
    nationalism and, 20
    results of, 17–18
    in software and IT support, 35

Pacific Railroad Acts, 74
patents, 76–77
peer review, 129
Perot, Ross, 36
personal computers, 48
Personal Knowledge (Polanyi), 56
photovoltaic cells, 8–13, 50, 52,
    80, 141–143
Polanyi, Michael, 56
Porter, Michael, 25, 42–43, 55, 107
postindustrial society, ix, 2–3
    competitiveness through services
    in, 42–44
Pratt & Whitney Company, 46
precision machining, 84
President's Council of Advisors on
    Science and Technology, 127
Prestowitz, Clyde, 37
Principles of Economics (Marshall), 53
private returns, 58–60
process innovation, 2, 62–63
    maturity of process and, 63,
    65–69, 109–111, 114–115
    modularity and, 63–65, 109–111
    product components and, 70–72
    pure, 67
    science in, 126–128
process-technology life cycle,
    113–114
product design, 63–65
    advantage of low modularity in,
    114–115
    components in, 70–72
    location decisions and, 111–112

production processes, modularity
of, 64–65, 109–111
productivity, x, 23
American system of
manufactures and, 46
in competitive advantage, 25
hopes pinned on increasing,
38–42
labor, 38, 39–42
measurement and analysis of,
39–40
policy to increase, 121
total factor, 38–39
protectionism, 6, 36–38, 88
proximity, 52–57
purpose, uniformity of, 24

Qualcomm, 66–67, 83

rare-earth elements, 11
RCA, 8
R&D. *See* research and
development (R&D)
recombinant DNA protein drugs, 64
research and development
(R&D), 2
basic and applied science in,
77–80, 90, 123–126, 125–126
businesses in erosion of, 90–95
creation of corporate, 76, 77
evaluating costs of separating,
109–115
government funding of, 77–80,
89–90, 123–126
interdependence of with
manufacturing, 62–69
international comparisons in,
86–88
jobs in, 79

labor markets for, 35
manufacturing links with, 15
maturity of processes and, 63,
65–69
modularity of, 63–65, 109–111
number of jobs in, xi
outsourcing, 17, 35
proximity of to manufacturing,
52, 60, 61–72, 103, 107–115
World War II, 77–79
Restoring Our Competitive Edge
(Hayes and Wheelwright), ix
returns, private versus social, 58–60
reverse engineering, 114–115
Ricardo, David, 24
Rivkin, Jan, 107
Roche/Genentech, 68–69
Roosevelt, Franklin Delano, 78
Russia, 29–30, 34–36, 85, 86

Sanofi, 24
Sanyo, 9–10
*Save Your Job, Save Our Country: Why
NAFTA Must Be Stopped—
Now!* (Perot), 36
science, technology, engineering,
and mathematics (STEM)
education, 131–133
*Science and Engineering Indicators
2012*, 6
Seiko Epson, 71
semiconductor manufacturing, 12
capabilities from, 14, 49, 52
clustering in, 55
"fabless" 66–67, 81, 83–84
on modularity–maturity index,
66–67
rise and decline of commons in,
80–84

services, 2–3
  competitiveness via, 42–44
  digitization of, 5
  trade deficit and, 4–5
  wealth in consumption of, 43
shared complementary assets, 58–59
shareholder interests, 103
Sharp, 9–10
Sherman Antitrust Act, 76
shoe production, 56
Sinsheimer, Robert, 128
social networks, 57
social returns, 58–60
solar photovoltaic cells, 8–13
Solyndra, 123
Sony, 71
Spence, Michael, 32–33, 43, 97
spillovers, 53, 91
steam locomotives, 48
steel industry, 113
Stevens Institute of Technology, 76
stock buybacks, 91–95
Strategic Computing Initiative, 125
strategy, 73, 103, 108–109
  capability building and, 104–107
  national, 119–133
  objectives of for manufacturing,
    121–122
structural shifts, 84–88
subsidies, 81–82, 122–123, 133
suppliers, 108
supply–demand linkages, 47, 58–59
supply push linkages, 49, 51
synthetic fuels program, 122–123

Taiwan Semiconductor
    Manufacturing Company,
    67, 83
targeting, 122–123, 127–128

taxes, 81–82, 120, 122–123, 124, 133
technology
  balance of trade and, 7–8
  board knowledge of, 117
  general-purpose, 51–52
  government policy on, 121,
    126–130
  international comparisons in,
    86–88
  manufacturing commons based
    on, 75–77
  post–WWII, 77–79
  rejuvenating manufacturing,
    113–114
Texas Instruments, 79, 81, 82, 83
total factor productivity, 38–39
Toyota production system, 57, 107
tradable sectors, 32–33
trade. See also free trade
  balance of, 3–5, 135
  barriers to, 6, 36–38, 55, 88
  comparative advantage theory
    on, 24
  competitiveness in international,
    23–24
  deficits, x, 19
  global expansion of, 30–33
  government policy on, 120
training, on-the-job, 132–133
transistors, finFET, 69
transportation systems, 74
trend analysis, 112–115, 128–130
2008 Solar Technologies Market
    Report, 9
Tyson, Laura D'Andrea, 25

United Kingdom, 7
United Microelectronics
    Corporation, 83

US Census Bureau, 27
US Department of Defense, 18, 125
US Department of Energy, 18, 129

value added, 2
  globalization and, 85
  manufacturing as low in, xi–xii
  per worker, 41
  trade balance and, 6–8
Varian, 8
vertical integration, 96
very large-scale integrated (VLSI)
    circuits, 82
vocational schools, 132–133

wages, x. *See also* living standards
  competitiveness and, 25, 29
  productivity correlated with, 38
  stagnation in real, 33

Watson, James, 128
Westinghouse, 76, 77
Wheelwright, Steven, ix
Wizard of Oz, The (movie), 135
workforce, 14–15. *See also*
    education; labor markets
  global increase in, 29–30
  skilled, 23, 33–36
  strategic value of, 108
  training, 132–133
  uniformity of purpose in, 24
World 3.0 (Ghemawat), 55
World Bank, 7
World Is Flat, The (Friedman),
    54–55
World War II, 77–79

Zegna, 115
Zysman, John, ix

About the Authors

GARY P. PISANO is the Harry E. Figgie, Jr. Professor of Business Administration at Harvard Business School, where he has been on the faculty since 1988. His research has focused on technology and operations strategy, outsourcing, R&D performance, the management of innovation, and competitive strategy. He is the author of over seventy-five research articles and case studies and the recipient of numerous awards, including the 2009 McKinsey Award for best article published in *Harvard Business Review*. His previous books have examined the evolution of business models and innovation in the biotechnology industry (*Science Business: The Promise, the Reality, and the Future of Biotech*), the link between capabilities and strategy (*Operations, Strategy, and Technology: Pursuing the Competitive Edge*), and process technology development (*The Development Factory: Unlocking the Potential of Process Innovation*). Pisano has advised senior executives at leading companies in the United States and Europe in a wide range of manufacturing and service industries. In addition, he serves on the boards of a number of start-up companies. He holds a BA in economics from Yale and a PhD in business administration from the University of California, Berkeley.

WILLY C. SHIH is Professor of Management Practice at Harvard Business School, where he has been on the faculty since 2007. He teaches in both the MBA and the Executive Education programs. His research is focused on technology strategy, capability acquisition in emerging market firms, and regional competitiveness.

Shih is the coauthor, with Gary Pisano, of "Restoring American Competitiveness," winner of the 2009 McKinsey Award. He is the author of over seventy papers and HBS cases. Prior to his current position, he held executive positions at IBM, Digital Equipment Corporation, Silicon Graphics, Eastman Kodak, and Thomson SA. He has led the building of billion-dollar businesses and now serves on the boards of several companies. Shih holds SB degrees in both chemistry and life sciences from the Massachusetts Institute of Technology and a PhD in chemistry from the University of California, Berkeley.